About the author

Gill Robins is an educational consultant and writer who received the UKLA John Downing Award for creative and innovative approaches to teaching English in 2010. She worked as a deputy head in the primary sector until 2011 and is also an experienced children's worker in a church context, including Sunday school teaching, weekday clubs and summer camps. Her published works include *The Whoosh Book*, a collection of literacy activities for classic and contemporary text for 7- to 14-year-olds (Routledge, 2013).

Praise for *The Whoosh Bible*

Wow—I wish I had had a copy of **The Whoosh Bible** when I was a school teacher. Storytelling is an integral element of the Christian faith and **The Whoosh Bible** offers a way of interacting with Bible stories that children will love. One of its most endearing features is that it can become a regular practice that will draw children into the text and help them to experience as well as understand its meaning. This is an indispensable resource for both church and school.

TREVOR COOLING, PROFESSOR OF CHRISTIAN EDUCATION, CANTERBURY CHRIST CHURCH UNIVERSITY

Human beings of all ages are story-makers. **The Whoosh Bible** is a groundbreaking new resource written for story-making children and those who teach and learn with them in churches and schools. It can provide them with a way to walk into the stories of the Bible and live in them and thereby to find meaning for the stories of their own lives. I look forward to the day when whooshing the narratives of scripture becomes a familiar activity in school and church.

JOHN SHORTT, SENIOR ADVISER, EUROPEAN EDUCATORS' CHRISTIAN ASSOCIATION, AND PROFESSORIAL FELLOW IN CHRISTIAN EDUCATION, LIVERPOOL HOPE UNIVERSITY

Barnabas for Children

Barnabas for Children® is a registered word mark and the logo is a registered device mark of The Bible Reading Fellowship.

Text copyright © Gill Robins 2015
The author asserts the moral right to be identified as the author of this work

Illustrations Rebecca J Hall 2015

Published by
The Bible Reading Fellowship
15 The Chambers, Vineyard
Abingdon OX14 3FE
United Kingdom
Tel: +44 (0)1865 319700
Email: enquiries@brf.org.uk
Website: www.brf.org.uk
BRF is a Registered Charity

ISBN 978 0 85746 380 7

First published 2015
10 9 8 7 6 5 4 3 2 1 0
All rights reserved

Acknowledgements
Unless otherwise stated, scripture quotations are taken from the Contemporary English Version of the Bible published by HarperCollins Publishers, copyright © 1991, 1992, 1995 American Bible Society.

A catalogue record for this book is available from the British Library

Printed by Gutenberg Press, Tarxien, Malta

THE WHOOSH BIBLE

GILL ROBINS

50 INTERACTIVE BIBLE STORIES FOR CHILDREN'S GROUPS

> Get rid of the frogs...
> I'll let God's people go!

Acknowledgements

We would like to thank Professor Joseph Winston of the University of Warwick for permission to use his original concept of a Whoosh.

Important information

Photocopying permission

The right to photocopy material in *The Whoosh Bible* is granted for the pages that contain the photocopying clause: 'Reproduced with permission from *The Whoosh Bible* by Gill Robins (Barnabas for Children, 2015) www.barnabasinchurches.org.uk', as long as reproduction is for use in a teaching situation by the original purchaser. The right to photocopy material is not granted for anyone other than the original purchaser without written permission from BRF.

The Copyright Licensing Agency (CLA)

If you are resident in the UK and you have a photocopying licence with the Copyright Licensing Agency (CLA) please check the terms of your licence. If your photocopying request falls within the terms of your licence, you may proceed without seeking further permission. If your request exceeds the terms of your CLA licence, please contact the CLA directly with your request. Copyright Licensing Agency, Saffron House, 6–10 Kirby Street, London EC1N 8TS, email cla@cla.co.uk; web www.cla.co.uk. The CLA will provide photocopying authorisation and royalty fee information on behalf of BRF.

BRF is a Registered Charity (No. 233280)

Scripts can be downloaded at www.barnabasinchurches.org.uk/9780857463807

Contents

Introduction 7

Old Testament stories

1	How it all began	10
2	Adam and Eve	13
3	Noah's boat	16
4	Abraham goes into the unknown	19
5	Rebekah, a wife for Isaac	22
6	Jacob and Esau	25
7	Joseph's coat and ten jealous brothers	28
8	Joseph in Egypt	31
9	Moses: prince, shepherd and leader	34
10	Let my people go!	37
11	Crossing the Red Sea	40
12	The grumbling Israelites	43
13	Joshua: a new leader	46
14	Joshua and the walls of Jericho	49
15	Gideon leads God's people	52
16	Samson the strong man	55
17	Ruth chooses a family	58
18	Hannah's baby	61
19	David fights a giant	64
20	Solomon makes wise choices	67
21	God cares for Elijah	70
22	Elijah and the prophets of Baal	73
23	Naboth's vineyard	76
24	Elijah and Elisha, prophets of God	79
25	Jonah and the people of Nineveh	82
26	Jeremiah is given a special job	85
27	Nebuchadnezzar builds a big fire	88
28	Daniel in the lions' den	91

| 29 | Esther saves the day | 94 |
| 30 | Nehemiah rebuilds a wall | 97 |

New Testament: the life of Jesus

31	Elizabeth and Zechariah	102
32	Jesus is born	105
33	Jesus meets John the Baptist	108
34	Jesus in the wilderness	111
35	Jesus' last week	114
36	Jesus is risen	117

New Testament: stories Jesus told

37	The good Samaritan	122
38	The lost son	125
39	The lost sheep	128
40	Building work	131
41	The sower	134
42	Planning ahead	137

New Testament: people Jesus met

43	Special friends	142
44	The wedding at Cana in Galilee	145
45	Learning to trust	148
46	Feeding 5000 people	151
47	Healing the blind	154
48	Jesus heals more people	157
49	Being humble	160
50	The woman at the well	163

Colouring-in pages **167**

Introduction

We all love stories, whether telling our own stories by talking, texting and blogging or hearing the stories of others via newspapers, magazines and other media. Stories are the way we make sense of the world, our place in it and our relationships with other people. It is no surprise, therefore, that Jesus taught about the kingdom of God by telling stories to the crowds of people who followed him everywhere he went. In its entirety, the Bible is, of course, the story of God and his relationship with us, initially through the people of Israel and latterly through his Son, Jesus Christ.

Effective storytelling involves understanding the mind of the person to whom the story is being told, rooting the narrative in listeners' experiences so that they can access its meaning. Communicating the vastness of God's story to children therefore involves starting in the mind of the child, moving to the mind of God, and then returning to the mind of the child to root God's story in their experience. Whooshing is one way of doing this.

The Whoosh was created by Professor Joseph Winston of the University of Warwick and it is now widely used to support children as they develop understanding of narrative, from ancient sagas to Shakespeare and contemporary novels. It is a form of physical storytelling in which key actions, objects and words are represented physically. It is much more than acting out the story: it means actually becoming the story.

To Whoosh, stand all the participants in a circle to create an open space. You act as the chorus master or conductor, reading the narrative and bringing people into the circle in turn to become a character or an object for the duration of that section of the Whoosh. When each section is complete, you say 'Whoosh' (as marked in the text) and everyone returns to their place in the circle, ready for the next part of the story. You can also say 'Whoosh' to bring action to an end if it is getting too noisy. In this way, everyone is involved at some point in the story and, because action is continuous around the circle, there are no starring roles. Its improvisatory nature means that children can focus on the story and its meaning.

Each Whoosh is divided into sections, with text emboldened where an action or object is suggested. A list of people, objects and sounds is provided at the beginning of each Whoosh, to give you some idea of the challenges that your storytellers will meet. Children are endlessly creative and will have no problem in becoming objects, buildings or characters in turn. You may, however, want to read through the story aloud first, giving everyone a chance to grasp its content before concentrating on the detail.

There are various ways of dealing with speech. You can read the line for the actor to repeat, you can allow children to improvise speech as suggested by the narrative, or you can use script sheets (these can be downloaded at www.barnabasinchurches.org.uk/9780857463807). To do this, print off the script for the Whoosh you are using, cut the script into strips and give the strips to the relevant participants to read when they enter the central space. Sometimes it might be suitable for everyone to be involved, including those in the outer circle.

Sound effects can be added: voices are usually the most effective medium. Props can also be used, although too many props detract from the action and slow it down.

Here's a brief overview of how it works:

- Form a circle with a large central performance space.
- Tell the group that everyone who wants to will get a chance to be part of the story.
- Start reading the story. When you reach a bold-type word, pause and gesture to a child to move into the centre of the circle, either to create a pose representing the object, or to mime the action of the character.
- Sometimes you will invite several children into the circle at the same time. Occasionally, everyone might be involved.
- When you say 'Whoosh', everyone returns to their original place in the circle.
- Move around the circle to invite actors for the next section of the story, so that everyone has a turn.
- Acting will become more confident with experience. Experienced whooshers can add props and improvise dialogue.

In the following Whooshes, the suggested objects are chosen for particular reasons because of their resonance in the story. An example is Moses' stick, chosen because it was an important symbol of God's power. There is even a challenge, in the story of Jesus in the desert, of creating physical representations of scorching heat and freezing cold. You or your children may want to emphasise other objects, which is fine, as long as the objects you choose are crucial to the story and it doesn't become too cluttered with action. Some of the Bible stories, most notably 'Joseph in Egypt' and 'Esther saves the day', have been abbreviated for ease of use and to make the Whoosh more effective.

Each story concludes with discussion starters (rooting the story back in the mind of the child), a craft activity which becomes a visual reminder of the story to take home, and a prayer. These are only suggestions, though. Your children may want to say their own prayers or discuss some aspect of the story not suggested in the discussion starters. Be flexible: children's questions are key indicators of their thoughts, so any questions they ask, even if they seem obscure to you, are relevant to their thinking about the story in a way that your questions are not.

Teachers and organisations that Whoosh find that the act of becoming the story gives children an understanding of its meaning in a way that nothing else does. Actions and words combined have a powerful effect not only on understanding but also on the detail that is remembered. Whooshes have a vital part to play in the sharing of God's story with children. Enjoy your Whooshing!

Some benefits of the Whoosh

- Children become active participants in the story.
- Whooshing is a circle activity in which everyone gets a go, regardless of age, ability or command of language.
- Roles change often during a Whoosh so that everyone is able to join in.
- Becoming characters and objects in the story encourages children to listen carefully and interact with each other.
- Whooshing is a safe medium within which to explore new ideas and experiment with new roles.
- It helps children to engage with the story and develop empathy with the characters.
- It's lots of fun!

Old Testament stories

1

How it all began

GENESIS 1:1—2:4

characters	objects	sounds
God	emptiness	roaring water
sea creatures	darkness	splashing waves
birds	earth	rustling leaves
animals	planets	whale songs
people	dark/night/evening	splashes from darting fish
	light/day/morning	noisy birds
	water/oceans	birdsong
	dome/sky	trumpeting elephants
	clouds	roaring lions
	dry ground/land	chattering monkeys
	waves/swells/troughs	
	different trees/plants/flowers	
	seeds	
	sun, moon and stars	

The first three sections of this Whoosh are very effective when lengths of flowing coloured fabric are used as props to represent the sea, sky and land as each one is created.

In the beginning, there was nothing. Just **emptiness**. Just **darkness**. Out of nothing, **God** decided to create the universe—our **earth** and all the other **planets**. At first, there was just a **roaring ocean** of water all around the earth. It was empty. And it was **dark**. So **God** created **light**, and he separated the **darkness** from the **light**. He called the **darkness** 'night' and the **light** 'day'. The evening came. It got **dark**. The **light** came again. It was morning. Day one!

WHOOSH

The **earth** was still completely covered in **water**. So next, **God** made a huge **dome**, with some of the **water** above it and some of the **water** below it. He called the dome 'sky', and he stored the **water** above the sky in **clouds**, ready for when the earth needed rain. The evening came again. It got dark. The **light** came again. Day two!

WHOOSH

The next morning, **God** collected together all the **water** that was under the **sky**, so that **dry ground** appeared. He called the **collected water** 'oceans' and the **dry ground** 'land'. Frothy **waves** broke and splashed gently on to the **land**. Far out in the deep **oceans**, the **water** rose and fell in **huge swells** and **deep troughs**.

'That's good,' said **God**. 'Now the land needs some plants.' And he completely covered the **dry ground** with every sort of plant. There were **trees with scented blossom**. There were **trees** with **fruit**. There were **giant trees** and **small trees**. There were **trees** with **smooth bark** and **trees** with **scratchy bark**. There were **plants** with **long, swishy leaves** that **rustled** in the breeze, and **plants** with **short, curly leaves**. There were **climbing plants** with **shiny leaves stretching up** to reach the light in the jungle, and there were even **tiny little plants** that covered the **ground** with carpets of beautiful **flowers** in the meadows. Every single plant had its very own **seeds** hidden away safely inside it, so that it was all ready to make brand new, identical plants.

'That's good,' said **God. Evening** came. **Morning** came. Day three!

WHOOSH

Next, **God** wanted to make some lights to put in the sky, to separate the day from the night. So he made two great big lights and then lots and lots of tiny stars. There was a **warm, glowing light** to shine brightly during the **day**, and a **smaller light** to shine with the **tiny star lights** at **night**. Then, **God** set the **earth** spinning and moving around the **lights**, so that they could even mark days, years and seasons.

'That's good,' said **God**, as **evening** and **morning** came. Day four!

WHOOSH

'The oceans and the skies need creatures to fill them,' said **God** next morning. So **he** created huge **whales** and **giant sea creatures** that lived far out in the **deep, deep ocean. He** created **shoals of little silver fish** that jumped and darted. He created **octopi** and **eels. He** created **sea horses** and **coelacanths. He** filled all the **seas** and **oceans** with **fish** and **creatures** of every kind. **He** filled the **skies** with different kinds of winged **birds**—**bright, noisy** ones to live in the **jungles, quiet wading birds** to live in the **water** and **tiny darting ones** with **chirpy songs** to live among the **plants**. As **evening** came, **God** blessed them all. Day five!

WHOOSH

On day six, **God** filled the land with all sorts of animals—**crawly insects; graceful giraffes with long, bendy necks; magnificent, trumpeting elephants; roaring lions; scampering, chattering monkeys** and **sleepy sloths**.

'That's good,' said **God**. But he hadn't quite finished. Although the land was full of animals, **God** thought it still needed something else. So **he** made **people**, to care for his brand new world. The **people** were different from the animals because **God** made them to be just like him. 'That's very, very good,' said **God** as the day came to an end.

And there was our beautiful world. There was just one day left in the week, and on day seven, **God** had a rest from all the work of creating that he had done.

WHOOSH

Follow up

Discussion

- What was it like when there was nothing but darkness? To experience this, make your room as dark as possible and try to imagine what it was like when there was nothingness and emptiness.
- Give each child a glow stick. At a given signal, all break your glow sticks to make light.
- Talk about the effect of light in the darkness.

Activity

- Divide the children into eight groups. Give each group a set of colouring materials (crayons or paints) and a piece of paper (A3 if space is limited, or a larger piece if there is space to work on the floor).
- Give each of the first seven groups one day of creation for which to produce a picture. The picture for the final group should be of a completed world, full of all that God created.
- Starting with one piece of plain black paper to represent darkness, put the pictures in order to create a panoramic sequence showing how God created the universe from nothing.

Prayer

Father, thank you for the beautiful world that you created for us to live in. Help us always to respect and care for it. Thank you that you created people to be your special friends. Amen

2
Adam and Eve

GENESIS 2:4—3:24

characters	objects	sounds
God people (Adam and Eve) angels	garden animals plants streams sunshine special tree snake Tree of Life flaming sword	splashing

The number of characters in this story is limited but, if you have a large group, you could create a garden scene with plants and animals at the beginning of each section of the Whoosh.

The **people** God created were his friends, and **he** made them a beautiful **garden**, called Eden, to live in. **They** loved their garden. There were lots of **animals** to play with and **plants** full of lush fruit for them to eat. They could **splash** in the bubbling **streams** or **sit** in the **sunshine** and rest. Then, in the evenings, as the air grew cool, **God** would visit his friends, **Adam** and **Eve**. They would **walk** together in the garden, looking at the **plants** and **talking** about what they had done that day. **They** would tell God the names that they had chosen for the **animals**.

In the middle of the garden, **God** had **planted** a **special tree**. It was special because anyone eating its fruit would suddenly know the difference between right and wrong. 'So please don't eat that fruit,' said **God** to Adam, **pointing** to the tree. 'If you do,' **he** added, 'you will die.'

WHOOSH

One of the animals who lived in the garden with them was a **snake**, and he was very, very crafty. Waiting until **Adam** and **Eve** were near the **special tree** one day, the **snake** slithered up to **Eve**.

'Did God really say you can't eat this fruit?' **he** grinned.

'God told Adam that we'd die if we touched it,' **Eve** answered.

'No you won't,' hissed the **snake**. 'God just doesn't want you to know everything that he knows.' The **snake** watched her, to **see** what she would do.

Eve looked at the **tree** and **walked** around it thoughtfully, **reaching out** a few times to touch some of the branches. God *had* said they could eat anything in their garden. And, after all, they *were* his special friends. Surely he wouldn't mind. The **snake** saw her hesitation. 'Try some,' **it** prompted, **getting** a little nearer to **her**. 'Go on, try some!'

Eve looked guiltily around, then slowly **reached** up, **pulled** off a piece of fruit and **tasted** it—carefully at first, then with bigger bites. It was *de–lic–ious*. It was the best fruit in the whole garden. Unnoticed, the **snake** slithered away to a safe distance and **watched** them.

WHOOSH

Eve held the fruit out to **Adam**.

'It's lovely,' **she** said. 'You try it.' And even though God had told him not to eat it, **Adam** took the fruit that **she** was **offering** him and took a bite. Grinning triumphantly, the **snake glided** silently away.

Suddenly, **Adam** and **Eve felt** something they had never felt before. They **felt afraid**, because they knew that what they had done was wrong. What was worse, their friend God would know what they had done, too. So **they** made a plan. **They hid.**

When **God** visited the garden that evening, **he** couldn't see them. **He** looked everywhere. **He** called out, 'Where are you?' then, 'Why are you afraid?' and then, sadly, 'Have you eaten the fruit?'

WHOOSH

Adam and Eve felt very ashamed as they **crept** out from their **hiding place** with their heads down. **They** couldn't bear to look at **God** now that they had been so disobedient. Would he still be their friend?

'Why did you eat it?' **God** asked Adam.

'The woman you gave me told me to,' said **Adam, pointing** at Eve.

'Why did *you* eat it?' **God** asked Eve.

'The snake you made and put in our garden told me to,' **she** answered, **looking around** for the snake to blame.

God was very sad. Adam and Eve had spoiled their friendship and ruined the future that he had planned for them. Nothing would ever be the same again. **Adam** and **Eve** had to leave the beautiful garden for ever. **Adam** had to work hard to **grow** his own food. **Eve** couldn't play with the animals any more. **Some** of them **were afraid** of her. **Some** of them had become **dangerous** and **they** would **fight** with each other, so **Eve** was afraid of them.

And worst of all, **they** had spoilt their friendship with **God**. Because they had been disobedient, **they** knew that when they got old, they would **die**.

WHOOSH

There was still one **special tree** in the **garden** that nobody had touched. It was the Tree of Life. Anyone eating the fruit from this tree could live for ever, so **God** put **angels** at the **entrance** of the garden to guard the tree, and a **flaming sword** that continually **flashed** back and forth. Nobody could ever go into the **garden** again.

WHOOSH

Follow up

Discussion

- What was the conversation before the forbidden fruit was taken?
- Why did people choose to do something that they had been told not to do?
- Why do we do things that we know are wrong?
- What is temptation?
- How do we feel when we are disobedient?
- How might making wrong choices affect our friendships?
- How does God feel?

Activity

This activity could be used at the start of the session, before the story is introduced.

- Place various plates on a table, each containing enough pieces of fruit for everyone to have some. Place one bowl centrally, containing pieces of a particularly tempting fruit. Tell your group that you are going to leave the room for a couple of minutes and nobody is to touch this fruit.
- Leave the room, but stay within earshot so that you hear the conversation. Return to the room after a few minutes. How many people have touched the forbidden fruit?

Prayer

Father, I am sorry for the times when I have been disobedient. Thank you that you have promised to forgive me and to help me make the right choices in future. Amen

3

Noah's boat

GENESIS 6:1—9:17

characters	objects	sounds
God	enormous boat	sawing
people	window	hammering
Noah	roof	rain
Ham, Shem and Japheth	three decks	splashing waves
four wives	door	wind
neighbours	animals and birds	lapping water
	waves	
	mountain tops	
	raven	
	dove	
	falling flood waters	
	sunshine	
	rainbow	

When **God** made the world, complete with people to care for it, **he** was **pleased** because everything was very good. But then **God** became **sad**, because the **people** who lived on the earth changed and they weren't the way he'd created them any more. **They hurt** each other. They **fought**. They **stole** and they were **unkind**. Once, people had been God's special friends, but now **they** just **ignored him**. **God's** heart was broken by what **he saw**. So **he** made a decision.

There was just **one man** on the earth who loved **God**. His name was **Noah**. 'I'm going to start again,' **God** told **Noah**. 'I'm going to send a huge flood that will kill all the bad people.'

WHOOSH

But God promised **Noah** that he and his family would be OK. God had a plan. **He** told **Noah** to build an **enormous boat** that would keep him safe while the flood washed the earth clean of all its badness. So, even though it seemed a strange thing to do, **Noah** trusted God. **He** and his three sons, **Ham**, **Shem** and **Japheth**, started work, drawing plans, measuring, **sawing** and **hammering**. As **they** worked, their **wives** brought them food and **marvelled** at the huge **boat**, which was bigger than anything anyone had ever seen before. It was made of wood, with a **window**, a **roof**, **three decks** and a **door** in the side. Noah's **neighbours scratched** their heads and wondered what on earth he was up to. Eventually it was finished, and the **men** stood back and looked at their handiwork.

WHOOSH

The **boat** was ready. Next, **God** told **Noah** to put two of every kind of **animal** and **bird** on the **boat**, together with food and all that they would need. What a kerfuffle there was as the **animals** all lined up in their pairs to get on board. **Noah** and his **family** trusted God and did as he said, so **they** were very busy **getting** everything ready, **preparing food** and then **carrying** it all on to the boat. Finally, **Noah**, his **wife**, his **three sons** and their **wives** all went into the **boat** and **God** closed the **door**.

And then the heavens opened. It **rained**. And it **rained**. And it **rained** some more. Raindrops **drummed** on the roof of the **boat. Waves splashed** and **sloshed** against the side of the **boat**. It **rained** for days and days. It didn't stop raining until the highest **mountain tops** had disappeared under water. Only **Noah**, his **family** and the **animals** were left alive as **their boat floated** on the water. God really did want to wash his beautiful world clean.

WHOOSH

Then suddenly, one day, the **noise** of the rain **stopped. Everyone** stood still where they were and **listened**. There was a different noise now—the noise of **wind**. The **boat** still **drifted**, and the **water** still **lapped** against the sides, but it was a much gentler sound. And at least there was no more rain. After a while, they felt the **boat shudder** to a stop. When **they** looked out of the **window**, they could see **mountain tops** all around them. Their **boat** was stuck on **top** of a **mountain**!

After 40 days, **Noah** opened the **window** and sent out one of the **ravens**, but it couldn't find anywhere to land, so it just kept **flying** back and forth. Then he sent out a **dove**, but it couldn't find anywhere to land either, so it came back to the **boat**. But seven days later, when **Noah** sent the **dove** out again, **it came back** with an olive branch in its beak. So **Noah** knew that the **flood waters** were **falling**.

WHOOSH

But **Noah** still **waited**—for another **seven** days. And this time, when **Noah** sent the **dove** out, it didn't come back, so **he** knew that it was safe to leave the **boat** at last. As his **family** and all the **animals streamed out** into the warm **sunshine, Noah** knelt down to thank **God** for keeping them safe.

God promised never to flood the earth again, and, as a sign of his promise, he put a huge **rainbow** in the sky. **God** said, 'Never again. This is my promise to you.'

Noah, Ham, Shem, Japheth and their **wives** looked at the beautiful colours spanning the sky and they knew that every time clouds covered the sky and a rainbow appeared, God would remember his promise to his friends and to all living things.

WHOOSH

Follow up

Discussion

- Why was God sad about the behaviour of the people he had created?
- What things do we do that make God sad?
- Why did God put a rainbow in the sky?
- What promise did he make to Noah and his family?
- What does God's promise mean to us?

Activity

- Using a circle of white card (paper plates are ideal), colour or paint the lower half of the plate blue, to represent the flood water. Then, using any medium (scrunched-up tissue paper, coloured rice, ribbon, and so on), create a rainbow on the upper half of the plate.
- Write the words 'God has promised' centrally on the plate, followed by the name of the child.
- If both sides of the plate are decorated, a string can be added to create a hanging, twirling reminder of the story of Noah.

Prayer

Father, thank you that you made a promise never to flood the world again and that you remember your promise every time a rainbow appears in the clouds. Thank you that you love me and you forgive me when I do things that make you and other people sad. Help me to trust you, just like Noah did. Amen

4

Abraham goes into the unknown

GENESIS 12:1–9; 15:1–7; 18:1–14; 21:1–7; 22:1–13

characters	objects	sounds
Terah	tents	
Haran and wife	cattle	
Nahor and wife	sky	
Abraham	sun	
Sarah	shady tree	
family	donkey	
Lot	mountain	
friends	ram	
God	thorny bush	
three men		
servants		
Isaac		
voice		

God had sent a flood across the whole world. After the water dried up, Noah and his sons, who had been saved from the flood, settled down with their families. About 300 years after the flood, a man called **Terah**, one of Noah's many descendants, had three sons, called **Haran**, **Nahor** and **Abraham**. The **boys** grew up and **married**. But while both of his brothers had children, **Abraham** and his wife **Sarah** often felt sad because they had no children of their own.

Then one day, **God** said to **Abraham**, 'Leave your friends. I want you to go to another country.' Abraham trusted God, so, even though he was 75 years old, and even though it meant leaving their **family** and **friends, Abraham, Sarah** and their nephew **Lot** set out on a journey into the unknown. All they knew was that God was going to give them a new country of their own and they were going to be his people.

'I will make you into a great nation,' promised **God**.

WHOOSH

They travelled through country after country, **pitching** their **tents** for a while before **moving on**. **Abraham** and **Lot** gradually became very wealthy, owning lots of **cattle**, silver and gold. Eventually, they owned **so many cattle** between them that there wasn't enough grass to go around. So Abraham and **Lot** agreed to part company and **they** went their separate ways.

One night, **Abraham** was **sitting** and **thinking** about what God had said before they left on their journey into the unknown. **He** wondered how he could be part of a new nation of people when he had no children. But while he was wondering, **God** told him to **go outside** the **tent** and look up at the **sky**.

'Can you count the stars?' asked **God. Abraham** tried. When **God** saw that Abraham couldn't, **he** said, 'Your family will be like the stars—too many for you to count.' **Abraham** didn't know how it was going to happen, but **he** trusted God that it would.

WHOOSH

Another day, **Abraham** was **sitting** in his **tent, sheltering** from the blistering midday **sun**, when he saw **three men walking** towards him. 'Join us,' **he** called out to them, 'and have something to eat and drink.' While the **visitors rested** under a **shady tree** with **Abraham, Sarah** and the **servants** got busy baking bread, roasting meat and bringing milk for the **visitors** to drink.

'Where's Sarah?' **one of the visitors** asked as they were eating.

'There, in the tent,' answered **Abraham**.

'She's going to have a baby,' **one of the visitors** said.

Sarah was standing at the entrance to the tent. When she heard this, **she** just **laughed**. She was far too old to have a baby.

WHOOSH

But, just as the men had said, **Sarah** did have a **baby**, even though she was very old. **Abraham** called him **Isaac**, and when he was born, **Abraham** and **Sarah** were both happier than they had ever been before. **Abraham** provided a big feast for **everyone**, to celebrate. **God** had kept his promise.

As **Isaac** grew up, his **parents** were very proud of him and loved him very much. But God wanted to make sure that Abraham really did trust him, even with the most precious gift he had ever been given.

So **God** told **Abraham** to take his **donkey** and set out on another journey. **Abraham** left early the next morning, taking just **Isaac** and **two** trusted **servants. Sarah** was left at home in her **tent**. It took three days to get to the **mountain** where God had told Abraham that he was to sacrifice his son. **They stopped** once and **cut** enough wood to build an altar, before **going on their way**.

WHOOSH

When **they** arrived at the **mountain, Abraham** told the **servants** to stay with the **donkey** while **he** and **Isaac** went to pray. 'Father,' said **Isaac** as **they** piled up the wood to build the altar, 'we have wood and fire. Where is the sacrifice?'

'God will provide it,' said **Abraham** quietly as **he** took a rope and **bound Isaac** to the altar.

Suddenly **a voice** called, 'Abraham. Abraham.'

'Here I am,' **he** answered.

'Don't hurt your son,' **the voice** said. As **Abraham** looked up, he saw a **ram** trapped by its horns in **a thorny bush. He** untied his **son** and together they killed **the ram** and burnt it as their sacrifice. They **thanked God** for caring for them. **Abraham** looked up at the sky and remembered God's promise that there were going to be more people in his family than there were stars in the sky or grains of sand on the beach.

God made this promise because he knew that Abraham was willing to trust him. Abraham had proved it by even being willing to give God the life of his own son.

WHOOSH

Follow up

Discussion

- What did God promise Abraham about his family?
- Why was Abraham unsure about how this could happen?
- What other things had happened in his life that helped him to trust God to keep this promise?
- How can learning about Abraham's faith help us to trust God?

Activity

- Cut a star shape out of card, using a template, or use pre-cut stars.
- Write your name in the centre of the star as a reminder that each of us is a member of God's family. Tape a safety pin to the back of the star to make a badge.
- Glue together several stars of different sizes and colours to make a starburst badge.

Prayer

Thank you, Father, that I belong to your family—a family that has more people in it than there are stars in the sky. Amen

5

Rebekah, a wife for Isaac

GENESIS 24

characters	objects	sounds
Isaac	sheep	moaning and growling
Abraham	cattle	camels
family	donkeys	
servants	camels	
Canaanite girls	well	
girls at the well in Haran	Rebekah's home	
Rebekah		
Rebekah's mother		
Rebekah's father		
Laban		
maids		

Abraham and **Sarah** were sometimes sad, because they thought they would never have children, even though God had promised Abraham that there would be more people in his family than there were stars in the sky. But when they were old, they had a son. **Isaac** grew into a strong young man, and his father **Abraham** was blessed in many other ways, too. He had **sheep, cattle, donkeys** and **camels**, as well as silver and gold. He and his **family** were looked after by lots of **servants**. But **Abraham** was getting very old and he wanted Isaac to have a wife to share his life.

   Abraham thought about his home town: many years had passed since he had left. He was living far away in Canaan, but he knew that Isaac couldn't marry any of the local **girls**. He had to marry someone who worshipped God—someone from his family back in Haran. So one day **he** called his most trusted **servant** to him and **asked him** to go on a long journey, back to Haran, to find a wife for his son.

   'What if she doesn't want to come back here with me?' **asked** the **worried servant**, but **Abraham** reassured him that God had everything under control. So off went the **servant**, with **ten camels** loaded with gifts for Abraham's family.

WHOOSH

The **servant**'s long, weary journey was coming to an end one evening when he **spotted** a water **well**. The tired **camels** were all **moaning** and **growling**, so, **sliding** gratefully to the ground, the **servant** made all the **camels kneel down** to rest for a while before finishing their journey. He needed a rest, too, but he was thirsty, so he **wandered** to the **well**, **watching** all the **girls** from the town **bringing** their pots and **filling** them with water for their families. **He** was **praying** about how he would know whether one of these girls was the one that God wanted Isaac to marry, when **he** had an idea. He would ask one of the girls for a drink, and, if she offered to get water for his camels too, then that would be the girl for Isaac.

'May I have a drink?' **he** asked **Rebekah**, who had just arrived with her jar on her shoulder. As **she** gave him a drink, **she** said, 'Shall I get water for your camels as well?'

WHOOSH

Excitedly, the servant went back to his **kneeling camels** and, opening one of the packs that the **camels** were carrying, he took out rings and bracelets and gave them to **Rebekah**. **They** got talking while **she** was giving the camels their water, and it turned out that her grandad was actually Abraham's brother. So she was family! The **servant** told her all about Abraham, why Abraham had sent him to Haran, and how God had made it clear that Rebekah was the wife for Isaac.

While **he** was getting the **camels** ready to move on, **Rebekah** rushed home to tell her **mother** what had happened. As soon as he saw the rings and bracelets, Rebekah's brother **Laban** went out to meet the **servant** and welcome him to their **home**.

WHOOSH

The **camels** were fed, the **visitors** were given water to wash, and then **they** all sat down to a meal together. **Rebekah** and her **family** listened in amazement as the **servant** told them everything that had happened to Abraham since he had left Haran all those years ago.

At the end of the meal, Rebekah's **father** said, 'This is from God. Take Rebekah and go.' The **servant** gave Abraham's gifts to the **family**—clothes, silver, gold and jewellery for **Rebekah**, and other gifts for her **parents** and **Laban**, her brother.

WHOOSH

The next morning, **they** got ready for the long journey back to Canaan. **Rebekah** hurriedly **packed** her things, got her **maids** together and **prepared** to leave her family to go to her new home. **Laban** and **her parents** sent her on her way with a **prayer of blessing**, and then **she** left with the **servant**.

A few evenings later, back in Canaan, **Isaac** was walking in the fields alone, doing some **thinking**, when **he** saw some **camels** approaching. As a beautiful **young woman** got down from one of the camels, **Isaac** realised that this was the wife that God had chosen for him. **They** were soon married, and **Isaac** loved Rebekah very much.

Follow up

Discussion

- Why did Abraham want his son Isaac to marry someone from his own family, even though they lived a long way away?
- How did Rebekah care for the servant, even though he was a stranger?
- What does this tell us about the sort of person Rebekah was?
- Why do you think she agreed to leave her family and go back with the servant to marry Isaac?

Activity

This activity requires play dough, which can be made very easily:

- Mix 250 g plain flour with 50 g salt.
- Add 1–2 tablespoons of vegetable oil and 140 ml water.
- Knead until smooth.
- Use food colouring to colour as required, then store in the fridge until needed.

Roll out lengths of play dough into snakes. Then make a water pot by coiling the snakes of dough.

While they are working, remind children about how kind Rebekah was in offering water to a stranger. Also talk about why Abraham thought it was important that his son, Isaac, should marry a girl who worshipped the same God as he did.

Prayer

Father, please help me to be kind to people around me and to share what I have with other people. Thank you for my family. Thank you that I can belong in your family, too. Amen

6

Jacob and Esau

GENESIS 25:19–28; 27:1–46; 28:1–5, 13–30; 31:3–17; 33:1–5

characters	objects	sounds
Isaac	tents	
Rebekah	wild animals for hunting	
Jacob	domestic animals	
Esau	stars	
people	specks of dust	
Laban	stone	
Rachel	sheep	
Leah	cattle	
people at the wedding feast	goats	
Jacob's eleven sons		
Jacob's daughter		
Jacob's grandchildren		
servants		

Like his father Abraham before him, **Isaac** was blessed by God. He and his wife **Rebekah** had twin sons called **Jacob** and **Esau**. As the boys grew up, **they** started to enjoy doing different things: **Esau** loved to be outside and **he** became a skilful hunter. **He** was his father **Isaac**'s favourite. **Jacob** was quieter and loved to be at home around the **tents** where they lived. He was his mother **Rebekah**'s favourite. Sadly, as they grew up, **Jacob** and **Esau** became jealous of each other and **they** often argued.

WHOOSH

One day, when **Isaac** was very old, **he** called **Esau** to his **tent** and asked him to go **hunting** for meat so that Isaac could eat his favourite meal. **He** planned to give Esau God's blessing, because Esau was the older son. But **Rebekah** overheard, and, as soon as **Esau** was gone, she found **Jacob**. 'Quick,' **she** whispered. 'Cook your father's favourite meal, dress up as Esau, and get the blessing for yourself.'

So while **Esau** was out hunting, **Jacob** did just that. **He killed** one of his own animals, **cooked** a meal and **put on** some of Esau's clothes so that he smelt like his brother. Then **he** took the meal to his father's **tent**. Because **Isaac** was nearly blind, **he** put his hand on **Jacob**'s head and **gave him** God's blessing, thinking that he was Esau. When **Esau** got home, he also **cooked** a meal and **took** it to **Isaac**. It didn't take **them** long to realise that they'd been tricked, but **Isaac shook** his head sadly when **Esau** asked if he could take the blessing back. **Esau** was so angry that **he** promised to kill his

brother. When she heard that, **Rebekah** was worried, so **she** sent **Jacob** off on a long journey to live with her brother, Laban, in Haran, the town where she had grown up.

WHOOSH

As **he** fell asleep beneath the **stars** that night, **Jacob** was scared, because he knew that he had tricked God and lied to him as well as to his family. But he also knew that God would keep his promise to bless the person that Isaac had blessed. In a dream, **God** told Jacob that **he** was going to have a family with more people in it than there were **specks of dust**. The next morning, Jacob took the **stone** he had been using as a pillow and left it on the ground as a sign that he would trust and worship God.

When **he** arrived in Haran, **Jacob** was welcomed by **Laban** with open arms. **Jacob** started **working** in the fields, **caring** for the sheep, and it wasn't long before **he** fell in love with Laban's daughter, **Rachel**, who was a shepherdess. **He** asked **Laban** if he could marry her, in exchange for seven years' work without any pay. **Laban** was delighted.

The seven years seemed like a few days to Jacob, because he loved **Rachel** so much. And sure enough, after seven years, **Laban** arranged a huge **wedding** feast for **everyone**, to celebrate the marriage of his **daughter** and **Jacob**. But imagine **Jacob's** horror when the **bride removed** her veil and he discovered that he had been tricked into marrying Rachel's older sister, **Leah**! His uncle was an even bigger cheat than he was. He could only marry **Rachel**, the sister he truly loved, in exchange for another seven years' work.

WHOOSH

So there was **Jacob**, living in Haran with his **two wives**. As the years passed, **he** worked hard and grew rich. He had **big flocks** of sheep and cattle of his own, and his family grew, too. He had **eleven** strong sons, a **daughter** and, eventually, **grandchildren**.

Then, one day, **God** told **Jacob** that he was to return to Canaan, where he had grown up. So his **wives** and his **sons**, and their **wives** and **children, packed** their bags, **rounded up** all their **cattle**, and **left** Haran.

As they grew closer to the place where Esau lived, **Jacob** became more and more **worried**. Supposing Esau still wanted to kill him, even after all these years? **He** decided to send some of his **servants** ahead with a flock of **sheep** and **goats** as a gift for Esau.

But he needn't have worried. **Esau rushed** to meet him, **throwing** his arms around **Jacob's** neck and **welcoming** him home. **Esau** had forgiven **Jacob. He** had also become very rich and he, too, had lots of **cattle** of his own.

So the **two brothers** became **friends** again and **Jacob** and his **family settled** in Canaan.

WHOOSH

Follow up

Discussion

- The brothers were jealous of each other. How did their parents make this situation worse?
- Who were the cheats in this story?
- How did Jacob learn what it felt like to be cheated?
- Think about the end of the story. Which of the brothers got what they wanted?
- Why did God bless Jacob, even though he cheated?
- How did he bless Esau?
- Esau forgave Jacob. Why is it important to forgive?

Activity

- On a smooth, clean stone, write or draw something for which you would like to thank God.
- Pile the stones up and think about all the different ways that God cares for us.
- Return the stones to the children as a reminder that Jacob said 'thank you' to God by using a stone to mark the place where God had promised to bless him.

Prayer

Father God, sometimes I feel jealous of others or I get mad with people in my family when they aren't being fair. Help me always to be fair and to forgive people who hurt me. Amen

7

Joseph's coat and ten jealous brothers

GENESIS 37

characters	objects	sounds
Jacob	sheep	
Jacob's twelve sons	bundles of wheat	
Joseph, one of the sons	sun	
a man	moon	
Reuben, the oldest brother	stars	
Judah, a brother	flocks	
traders	home	
Jacob's daughters	well	
	camel train	
	animal	

Jacob lived in Canaan, the land where his father, Isaac, had always lived. He had a big **family**, with **twelve** strong sons. His eleventh son, **Joseph**, was born when Jacob was very old. **Joseph** used to help look after the **sheep** along with his **brothers**, but **he** often used to tell tales to his **father** about his brothers. Even so, **Joseph** was Jacob's favourite son. In fact, **Jacob** loved him so much that **he** made him a beautiful coat, covered in rich decoration. When **they** saw it, Joseph's ten **older brothers** were really jealous. In fact, **they hated Joseph** so much that **they** couldn't even **talk** to him without **scowling**.

Joseph wasn't very nice to **them** either. One night, **he** dreamt that **he** and his **brothers** were **tying up** bundles of **wheat** in the fields when **his bundle stood** upright and all his **brothers' bundles bowed** down to **his**. He not only dreamt it: **he told** his **brothers** all about it the next morning. That only made **them hate him** even more.

WHOOSH

Another night, **Joseph** had a different **dream**.

'Listen to this one,' **he** said gleefully to his brothers the next day. 'This time the **sun, moon** and **stars** were all bowing down to me.' His **brothers** were **furious** and even his **father** told him off this time.

One day, when the **ten older brothers** had **gone** to graze the **flocks**, some distance from **home**, **Jacob** told **Joseph** to **go** and **check up** on his **brothers** and the **sheep**, and then **come back** and **tell him** how they were. So off **Joseph** went, to the place where he thought they would be. When **he** got there, **he** had a good look around, but his brothers were nowhere to be seen.

'What are you looking for?' **a man** asked him.

'My brothers,' answered **Joseph**. 'Have you seen them?' The **man pointed** away into the distance, so off **Joseph** set again.

WHOOSH

His ten older **brothers saw Joseph** coming, long before he reached them. It gave **them** plenty of time to **plot** their revenge together.

'Here comes that dreamer,' **they sneered** as he got closer to them. **They** were so **angry** and **jealous** that **they** decided to kill **him, throw** his body down a **well** and then tell their father that a wild animal had killed his favourite son. **Reuben**, the oldest brother, was worried.

'Don't kill him,' he **pleaded** with his younger brothers. 'Just throw him down this well.'

So when **Joseph** finally reached **them**, that was what happened. **They grabbed him** and **took off** his coat, then they **picked him up** and **threw him** down a dry **well**.

Meanwhile, **Reuben** had gone off to see to the **flocks**. He planned to come back later, rescue Joseph and take him home safely. But while the **other brothers** were **eating**, a **camel train** passed them on its way to Egypt, and it gave **Judah** an idea.

WHOOSH

'Let's sell him,' **Judah** suggested. 'He could go and be a slave in Egypt.' It was no sooner thought of than done. **They** hauled **Joseph** up out of the **well, handed him over** to the **traders** and pocketed 20 pieces of silver. Then **they sat down** and **finished** their meal. So when **Reuben** returned to the **well** later, Joseph was gone.

Reuben was distraught. **He** was the oldest brother, so he was responsible for Joseph, and he knew how much their father loved him.

'What are we going to do now?' **he** yelled. 'What will father say?' The **brothers** needed to make up a story to explain Joseph's sudden disappearance, so **they tore** his beautiful coat, **covered it** in blood from an **animal, and started** to make their way **home**.

WHOOSH

When **they** arrived **home, they** gave the coat to **Jacob**.

'We found this,' **they** said. 'Isn't it Joseph's?' **Jacob** reached out and took his son's beautiful coat, all torn and covered in blood. **He** knew straight away that it was the one he'd given his son.

'He's been killed by a wild animal,' **he sobbed, hugging** the coat closely.

Jacob's heart was broken. **He cried** and **sobbed** day after day. His **daughters** tried to comfort him. His other **sons** tried to comfort him. But **Jacob** would not be consoled. His favourite son was dead.

WHOOSH

Follow up

Discussion

- Why do you think Joseph's brothers disliked him so much?
- How did their father Jacob make the situation worse?
- Joseph's brothers lied to their father about what had happened to Joseph. What effect did the lie have on Jacob?
- How do you think the brothers felt when they saw their father's sadness?
- How might their lies affect their relationship with their father in future?
- In this story, one thing led to another. Discuss how the problem got bigger and bigger, starting with favouritism and jealousy, and ending in lies about Joseph's death.
- What can we do when we feel that something isn't fair?

Activity

- Give each child the outline of a coat on A4 paper, or ask them to draw their own. Decorate the coat using any medium, so that it looks rich and colourful, and then cut out the coat.
- Like the children's game 'Pin the tail on the donkey', play 'Pin the coat on Joseph', challenging each child to recall a fact from the story before pinning their coat on a large outline of Joseph.

Prayer

Father God, even when Joseph and his brothers were lonely, scared or ashamed, you were there with them and you never forgot about them. Thank you that you are always with me, wherever I am, and that I can talk to you honestly, however I feel. Amen

8

Joseph in Egypt

GENESIS 39:1–6; 40:1—42:7; 45:1–7

characters	objects	sounds
Joseph ten older brothers slave traders Potiphar slaves and servants Potiphar's wife the king's butler the king's baker the king wise men people building grain stores scribes farmers people of Egypt Jacob and his family Benjamin	Potiphar's house prison seven thin cows seven fat cows	sawing hammering

When **Joseph** was just 17, his **brothers** sold him to **slave traders**. He was strong and handsome, and when he arrived in Egypt the **traders** sold him to **Potiphar**, an important official who was in charge of the king's guard. **Joseph** started his new life **working** as a slave in Potiphar's **house**, but **he** worked so hard and **got on** so well with his **owner** that eventually **he** became Potiphar's personal assistant. **He** was in charge of all the **slaves** and **servants**, running the house and all the fields that Potiphar owned.

Everything was going well. **Joseph** was an important and trusted person—until, that is, **Potiphar's wife** accused **Joseph** of trying to hurt her. Even though **he** was innocent and **he** kept saying so, **he** was thrown into **prison** and there **he** stayed, locked up with the king's **butler** and the king's **baker**. One night, the king's **butler** had a dream. In it, he saw a vine with three branches full of ripe grapes. **He squeezed** the grapes into the king's cup and **gave it to him** to drink.

'I can explain that,' said **Joseph** when he heard about the dream the next morning. 'It means that in three days you will be freed.' Sure enough, that is exactly what happened.

'Tell the king about me,' pleaded **Joseph** as the **servant** left prison, but as soon as **he** was free, **the servant** forgot all about Joseph.

WHOOSH

For two long years, **Joseph** stayed locked up **in prison**. Then, one night, **the king** had a terrible dream. In it, **seven thin cows** ate up **seven fat cows**. Frightened by what it might mean, **he called** his **wise men** to explain it. **They scratched** their heads and **consulted** their books, but, try as they might, **they** couldn't explain what it meant. Then the **butler**, who was standing nearby, suddenly **remembered Joseph**.

Quickly **Joseph** was brought from **prison. He** explained the dream: there were to be seven years of good harvests and seven years of famine. It was a **warning** from God that the Egyptians needed to prepare for famine by storing grain and food during the good harvests, so that nobody would starve during the bad years.

The king was so impressed with **Joseph** that **he** gave him a fine robe and a gold ring. **He** even made Joseph governor of all Egypt.

WHOOSH

Joseph set to work. **He travelled** all over Egypt on behalf of the king and, everywhere he went, the sound of **sawing** and **hammering** was heard as the **people built** store houses. **He** made sure that people stored spare grain. To start with, **scribes** recorded how much food was being harvested and stored by the **farmers**, but eventually there was so much that **they** couldn't count it all.

Then, just as God had said in the king's dream, the years of good harvest came to an end. **People** started to run out of food and **feel hungry**, so **Joseph** opened up all the **store houses** and **sold** food to the **Egyptian people**. Nobody went hungry.

WHOOSH

Meanwhile, back in Canaan, **Jacob** and his **family** were all slowly starving.

'Why are you just sitting here?' **Jacob** asked his **sons**. 'Go to Egypt and see if you can buy some grain.' Only **Benjamin**, Joseph's younger brother, was kept at home.

When the **brothers** arrived in Egypt, **Joseph** recognised them straight away, even though it was 15 years since he had last seen them. **They** didn't recognise him. While their sacks were being filled with grain by the **servants, Joseph** said nothing. But eventually **he** couldn't contain himself.

'Have everyone leave my presence!' **he** ordered. As soon as the room was empty, **Joseph** told his **brothers** who he was.

'Is Father still alive?' **he** asked, but the **brothers** were so terrified that not one of them could speak.

'It is really me,' **Joseph** assured them. 'Don't be afraid. God wanted me to come here.' And because he knew that there would still be another five years of famine before the harvests improved, **he** sent his **brothers** home to collect Jacob, the rest of the family and all their possessions.

WHOOSH

When **Jacob** heard the news, **he** set off for Egypt, hardly daring to believe that Joseph really was still alive. **Joseph** was watching for his father and, as soon as **he** saw **him** in the distance, **Joseph** had his chariot made ready and went out to meet **him. He** threw his arms around **his father** and **wept** for a long time.

The king met Joseph's **family**, and **he** told **Joseph** to let them live and graze their animals on the very best land that Egypt could offer. **Joseph** forgave his **brothers** for trying to harm him and **he** lived in Egypt with his **family** until **he** died at the age of 110.

WHOOSH

Follow up

Discussion

- How did Joseph become so important?
- How might he have reacted when his brothers arrived in Egypt?
- What do his forgiveness of them and his concern for his father tell us about him?

Activity

- Use a template to make a baseless pyramid—four triangles, with one of the triangles having a tab. (This template can be downloaded at www.barnabasinchurches.org.uk/9780857463807.)
- Cut around the outline of the shape, fold along the inside lines and use the tab to glue the pyramid together.
- Underneath each pyramid, put two or three biscuits for the children to share. This is a reminder that God provided food for Joseph and the Egyptians, and that Joseph shared the food with his brothers.

Prayer

Thank you, Father, that you provide food for us. Please help us to be generous and share with others. Amen

9
Moses: prince, shepherd and leader

EXODUS 1:15—4:28

characters	objects	sounds
Jacob	reeds	lapping water
eleven sons	River Nile	crying baby
other family	basket	baa-ing sheep
Joseph, the king's assistant	home	crackling flames
king of Egypt	royal palace	
new king	sheep	
Egyptian people	bush	
Israelite people	flames	
slave masters		
Israelite mum and dad		
baby boy		
Miriam		
princess		
maids		
Jethro		
Zipporah		
voice of God		
Aaron		

During a terrible famine in their own country, **Jacob, eleven** of his **sons** and all of their **families** had gone to live in Egypt, where **Joseph**, another of Jacob's sons, was an important assistant to the **king**. Over the years, their **families** had grown bigger and bigger, until **Israelite** people filled Egypt. Eventually, **Joseph** and all his **brothers** died, and so did the **king** for whom Joseph had worked.

The **Egyptian people** soon forgot that Joseph had saved them from starving to death during a long famine, and then a **new king**, who knew nothing about Joseph, **decided** that he had to do something about all the **Israelite people** living in his country. **He** was afraid that they might take over, so **he** put **slave masters** in charge of them.

Suddenly, all the **Israelite people** became slaves. **They** were forced to work hard, **making bricks, constructing buildings** and **working** in the fields from dawn until dusk. Just to be on the safe side, the **king** also gave an order for every **Israelite baby boy** to be killed as soon as he was born.

WHOOSH

But **one Israelite mum** couldn't bear the thought of her newborn **baby boy** being killed. For three months **she** cared for him at home, but when **she** couldn't hide him any longer, **she** made a little papyrus basket, **coated** it in tar to make it waterproof, **put** the baby inside it and **put** it among the **reeds** along the bank of the **River Nile**. The water **lapped** gently against the sides of the basket. The baby's older sister **Miriam** hid among the **reeds** to watch and see what happened.

It wasn't long before the king's **daughter** arrived. Her **maids** walked along the bank while the **princess** bathed in the **river**. Suddenly, **she** saw a little **basket** among the reeds. **She** sent one of her **maids** to fetch the **basket** and bring it to her. When **they** opened it, the **baby** inside started to **cry** and the **princess** felt very sorry for **him**. As **she** stood on the river bank, looking into the basket, **she** realised that he was a Hebrew baby who should have been killed when he was born.

Miriam, who had been hiding in the **reeds**, came along at just the right moment. 'I know someone who could look after him,' **Miriam** said to the **princess**. 'Shall I go and get her?'

And when the princess agreed, off went **Miriam** to fetch her **mum**. The **princess** handed over the **basket** with the baby still inside, and even **paid** his **mother** to look after him!

So the **baby** went back **home** and lived with his own **mum** and **dad**.

WHOOSH

All too soon, it was time for **him** to be taken to the **royal palace**. He became the **princess**'s son and **she** called him Moses. **He** grew up as an Egyptian **prince**, but he knew that he was Hebrew and he never forgot about his people. **He** was very sad when **he** saw **them** having to **work** so hard as slaves. One day, **he** was so angry about it that **he** killed one of the Egyptian **slave masters** and **buried** the body quickly, hoping that nobody had noticed. So, although he was a prince, **he** had no choice but to **run away** before the king found out what he had done.

He ended up working as a **shepherd** in a country far away, looking after **sheep** for a man called **Jethro**. Eventually, he married **Zipporah**, his boss's daughter, and they had a **son**. Meanwhile, back in Egypt, his **people** were **crying** out to **God** to save them from their suffering as slaves.

WHOOSH

One day, while **Moses** was listening to the **sheep** baa-ing, he saw a **bush** with **flames crackling** from it. Curious about why it wasn't burning up, **Moses** was going to have a closer look when a **voice** said, 'Moses. You are standing on holy ground.' So **Moses** took off his sandals and hid his face, because he knew that it was God who had spoken to him.

'I want you to go back to Egypt,' **God** said. 'I'm going to set my people free.'

Moses didn't think this was a particularly good idea. 'Why me?' **he** asked. 'Nobody will listen to me.'

But **God** said, 'Go. I will be with you.'

'I'm not really much good at talking,' **Moses** argued.

'Go,' said **God** crossly. 'I am your God. I will make the king of Egypt listen,' **he** promised.

So **Moses** went home to tell his **family** that they were going to Egypt. Meanwhile, **God** told Moses' brother **Aaron**, who was still living in Egypt, to **go** and meet Moses on his journey.

WHOOSH

Follow up

Discussion

- Why did Moses' mother hide him in a basket?
- What did God want Moses to do?
- God spoke to Moses from a burning bush. How can we know what God wants us to do?
- Why do you think that Moses argued with God about it?
- How might God's promise to Moses help us when we are facing something that we don't feel able to do?

Activity

- Cut an oval, about 8 cm in length, from brown paper, to represent the basket that Moses' mother made. Draw baby Moses on the basket and stick the basket on to a sheet of A3 paper.
- Draw around your hands several times on green paper. Cut out the hand shapes. Gluing just the palm parts of each hand, stick them around the basket. Leave the fingers of the cut-outs free to cover and hide the basket.

Prayer

Thank you, Father, that just as you were with Moses to help him free his people, so you will always be with me too. Amen

10

Let my people go!

EXODUS 4:29—12:32

characters	objects	sounds
God	River Nile	croaking frogs
Moses	stick	droning gnats
Aaron	palace	buzzing flies
Israelite leaders	frogs	drumming hailstones
Pharaoh	ovens	humming locusts
Israelite people	gnats	strong wind
Egyptian people	flies	
firstborn people and animals	animals	
Pharaoh's eldest son	houses	
	Egyptian crops	
	Israelite fields	
	locusts	
	total darkness	
	door frame	

This Whoosh contains plenty of opportunities to improvise sound effects, not only of the plagues themselves but also of the people's reactions to each of the plagues.

God told **Moses** and his brother **Aaron** to talk to the **leaders** of the Israelite people, so **they** called a meeting. **They** explained that God was going to free them from their slavery. When **they** heard this, the **leaders** knelt down and worshipped God because they were so relieved.

Next, **Moses** and **Aaron** went to **Pharaoh**. 'This is what God says,' **Moses** told him. 'Let my people go.'

'Why should I?' shrugged **Pharaoh**. 'I don't believe in your God.' And **he** made the **Israelite people** work even harder. **They** even had to collect the straw for the bricks they made. 'Lazy, that's what you are—lazy!' said **Pharaoh** when the **Israelites** complained.

So **God** told **Moses** to meet **Pharaoh** the next morning at the **River Nile**. When **he** got there, **Moses** stretched his **stick** out over the **river** and the water turned to blood. Right across Egypt, all the water turned to blood, even as **people** were pouring it out of their water jars. **Nobody** had any clean water.

Pharaoh just turned away and walked back into his **palace**. He wasn't going to listen to God.

WHOOSH

A week passed, then **Moses** and **Aaron** went to visit **Pharaoh** again. 'God says, "Let my people go!"' they told him. But **Pharaoh** wouldn't listen—that is, until **Aaron** stretched out the **stick** and **croaking frogs** came out of streams and rivers all over Egypt. **They** hopped into the **palace** and on to the king's bed. **They** jumped in the **ovens** and even into the food that the **people** were eating. 'Get rid of the frogs,' pleaded **Pharaoh**. 'I'll let God's people go.' But just as soon as the **frogs** were dead, **piled up** everywhere in stinking heaps, **Pharaoh** changed his mind. 'You can't go after all,' **he** told the **Israelites**.

WHOOSH

The next time **Aaron** stretched the **stick** out, **he** hit some dust from the ground. It turned into **droning** clouds of **gnats** that landed on **people** and **animals**, biting them.

The morning after that, **Moses** met **Pharaoh** again as he left the **palace** to go to the **River Nile**. 'Let my people go!' said **Moses**, but **Pharaoh** just ignored him. Suddenly, there were thick swarms of **buzzing flies** everywhere—in the **palace**, in **houses**, and even on the people's food.

'OK,' said **Pharaoh**. 'Stop the flies and I'll let you go.'

But just as soon as the **flies** had all gone, **he** changed his mind. 'Back to work,' he **snarled** at the **Israelites**. 'You aren't going anywhere.'

WHOOSH

'Let my people go!' said **Moses** to **Pharaoh** the next day.

'No!' said **Pharaoh**. So the **horses** and the **donkeys** and the **camels** and the **cattle** and the **sheep** and the **goats** that belonged to the Egyptians all **died**. The **animals** that belonged to the Israelites were fine.

'Let my people go!' said **Moses**.

'No!' said **Pharaoh**, and the next day, when **Moses** threw a handful of soot into the air, **everyone** was suddenly covered in sore, itchy boils. **People** were getting very grumpy.

WHOOSH

The day after that, there were **hailstones** drumming on the ground and flattening all the **crops** that grew in the Egyptian fields. But it didn't even rain on the **fields** where the Israelites lived.

'The men can go,' said **Pharaoh** eventually. A plague of **humming locusts** came and ate everything that was still left growing in the **Egyptians' fields**. The **people** looked worried. What would they eat?

'GO!' said **Pharaoh**. 'Just go. Please go.' But as soon as a **strong wind** blew the **locusts** away, **he** changed his mind. So **God** put **Egypt** into **total darkness** for three days.

WHOOSH

Because **Pharaoh** was still being stubborn, **God** brought one last plague. At midnight, the firstborn person in every family and the firstborn of every animal would be killed. **God** told the **Israelites** that each **family** should kill a lamb and put its blood on the **door frame** of their house. Then **they** had to roast the lamb, bake some bread and eat a meal. But **they** had to eat standing up, so that they were ready to leave.

And it happened exactly the way God said. The **firstborn person** in every family and the **firstborn** of every **animal** was killed—even the **king's eldest son**. Only those with the blood of the lamb painted on their **door frames** were spared. 'Go, quickly,' said the **Egyptians** the next morning. **They** even gave the **Israelites** their gold and silver as **the Israelites** left.

God's people were finally free.

WHOOSH

Follow up

Discussion

- What did God tell Moses to discuss with Pharaoh?
- God sent ten punishments because Pharaoh refused to free the Israelite people. How many can you remember?
- Why do you think Pharaoh kept changing his mind?
- Why did he eventually agree to let the people go? What had he learnt about God?
- What did the Israelite people have to do? What did they learn about God?

Activity

- Cut a strip of paper, 10 cm deep, from the long side of an A3 sheet of paper. Concertina-fold the strip into ten sections, each measuring 4 cm. Trim off the remaining 2 cm.
- Create a mini folding book by drawing a picture of one plague on each page of the book.

Prayer

Thank you, Father, that we can learn about you from stories of the Israelite people. Help me to trust you, even when things seem impossible. Amen

11

Crossing the Red Sea

EXODUS 13:17—14:30

characters	objects	sounds
God	desert	cheering
two or three people as 'they' for each section	thick cloud	grumbling Israelites
	flaming fire	strong wind
slaves making bricks	Red Sea	splashing water
soldiers	camp	roaring water
baby boys	Pharaoh's chariot	
Pharaoh	stick	
people of Israel	dry land	
sea	walls of water	
Pharaoh's officials	chariot wheels	
Egyptian army	daybreak	
Moses	torrent of water	
	broken chariots	
	beach	

This Whoosh works best with a couple of participants representing the people of Israel in each section. An actor representing God could remain in one part of the performance space throughout, demonstrating that God was always there. Involve everyone in the final section, either as a dead Egyptian or as a worshipping Israelite, so that the Whoosh ends with a large freeze-frame.

'Is it true?' **they** asked each other. 'Are we really free?' As **they** stood in the **desert**, their minds went back to the years of slavery in Egypt. They remembered those long hours in the burning sun, **making bricks**. They remembered the day when the **soldiers** had arrived to kill all their beautiful **baby boys**. And then they remembered how they had felt when they heard that **Pharaoh** had finally had enough. **He**'d decided to let them go and this time he had meant it.

So, here they were. True enough, **they** were ready for battle, as God had told them to be. Perhaps the Egyptians weren't going to make it easy for them, but they had escaped. **They** looked around at their **people**—God's people, free people. A **cheer** went up from everyone as **they** got ready to move.

WHOOSH

God had come to their rescue when they were slaves, and **he** was with them all the time, now that they had left Egypt. During the day, **he** went in front of them in a **big, thick cloud** stack that looked like a pillar. At night, when it was dark, the pillar became a **flaming fire** so that they could still see him. **They** were never alone, not in the day and not at night.

They knew they needed to cross the **Red Sea** before they were really safe, yet somehow **they** seemed to be going a very long way round. Sometimes, as **they** looked around, **they** even seemed to be going back on themselves. But **God** knew that although Pharaoh had let them go, he didn't really believe in their God, so **God** wanted to show the Egyptians who he was, once and for all.

He told the Israelites to make a **camp**.

WHOOSH

Meanwhile, back in Egypt...

'What have we done?' **Pharaoh's officials** moaned. 'We've got no slaves now.' **Pharaoh** ordered them to get his **chariot** and prepare the **Egyptian army** for a battle. **He** stood proudly in his **chariot** as he set off at the head of his **army**. He was going to get those slaves back if it was the last thing he did.

WHOOSH

In the distance, the **terrified Israelites** saw **Pharaoh** heading towards them. **He**'d changed his mind. **He** was coming to get them. There was nowhere to go. The **Egyptian army** would soon have **them** trapped by the **sea**. **They** forgot that **God** was caring for them as they panicked.

'We'd rather be slaves than die out in this desert,' **they** grumbled to **Moses**. 'Why didn't you leave us alone?'

'Don't be afraid,' answered **Moses**. 'Be brave.'

Then something strange happened. As the **Israelites** crowded forward to the edge of the **sea**, **Moses** stretched his **stick** out over the **water**. As night fell, the **huge cloud moved**, coming between the **Israelites** and the **Egyptians**. It was so dark behind the cloud that the **Egyptians** had to stop.

WHOOSH

Then, as the **Israelites** edged slowly towards the **sea**, **Moses** lifted up his **stick**. **God** sent **a strong wind** from the east. **Dry land** appeared where the sea had been and they walked through, with huge **walls of water** towering over them on either side. The wind blew all night as the **Egyptians**, seeing what was happening, started to follow them, but the **wheels** of their chariots got stuck and they couldn't move.

'Let's leave them alone,' **they** shouted to each other. 'God is on their side.'

WHOOSH

As **day** broke, with the **Israelites** safely back on land, **God** told **Moses** to stretch his **stick** out across the **water** again. As **he** did, the **water** rushed towards the trapped **Egyptians** with a roar. **They** tried to run away, but it was too late. A **torrent of water** drowned every last one of **them** and washed away their **chariots**.

WHOOSH

The **Israelite people** watched as **broken chariots** washed up on the **beach. They** knew that **God** had saved them, just as he promised he would. So **they all** worshipped **God**, right there on the beach, telling **God** that they trusted him and Moses.

WHOOSH

Follow up

Discussion

- What did the Israelites do when they met a barrier they couldn't cross? What did God do?
- How did they react when God saved them?
- What can we learn about God from the story? How can it help us to trust God?

Activity

- Make a model of the people of Israel crossing the Red Sea.
- Use a large piece of sand-coloured card as a base. Create walls of water from blue card, folding a tab along the bottom of each piece to secure it to the base.
- Give each child a piece of white card measuring 12 cm x 6 cm, on which to draw a picture of themselves. Leave 1 cm blank at the bottom of the card to use as a tab. Cut out each character, fold back the tab, and glue it in place on the model.

Prayer

Thank you, God, that you cared so much about your people that you saved them from the Egyptians. You were with the Israelite people all the time, and I know that you are with me all the time, too. Help me to trust you when there are things that I can't do. Amen

12

The grumbling Israelites

EXODUS 15:22—17:7; 19:1—20:18; 24:1–18; 32:1–35

characters	objects	sounds
Israelite people God Moses king of Egypt army guards Aaron	Red Sea animals water quails rock gushing water Mount Sinai cloud smoke fire golden calf	thunder lightning trumpet

The **Israelite people** had once been slaves in Egypt. Their lives were hard, but **God** heard their cries for help and sent **Moses** to the **king of Egypt** to persuade him to let the people go. For a long time, the **king** refused, but eventually **he** agreed to free them. And when **he** changed his mind and **tried** to get them back, all of his **army** drowned in the Red Sea.

But **God** kept the **Israelites** safe, and so here **they** were, by the shore of the **Red Sea**, with their **animals**, and their tents and everything they owned piled up on the beach. **They** worshipped God and **thanked** him for saving them. Then **they** set out on the long journey to their new home in another land.

WHOOSH

As **they** walked away from the sea shore and into the desert, **they** started to feel thirsty. **They** started to wonder what they were going to drink. After three days, **they** started to moan at **Moses**. Eventually they did find **water**, but when **they** tasted it, it was bitter and disgusting and **they** spat it out.

'What are we going to drink?' **they** complained. 'We're really thirsty.'

So **Moses** asked **God** what to do.

'Pick up a piece of wood,' **God** said, 'and throw it into the bitter water.' When **Moses** did as God said, the water became sweet and the **people** had long, refreshing drinks.

Soon it was time to move on again.

WHOOSH

They soon forgot how God had saved them from slavery, and how God had given them water to drink. As **they** walked, **they** moaned more and more.

'We're hungry,' **they** complained to Moses.

'We might as well have died in Egypt,' **some** said.

'Or at least stayed there,' **others** muttered. 'We had lamb stew and plenty of bread.'

'Have you brought us out here to starve to death?' still **more** moaned.

God heard them moaning, and he told **Moses** that he was going to send them food. So **Moses** called all the people together and explained that, during the evening, birds called **quails** would land in their camp and **they** could kill the birds for meat. In the morning, God would provide more bread than they could possibly eat.

WHOOSH

So that evening, **people** caught the **quails**. When **they** woke up the next morning, there was something that looked like thin flakes of frost covering the desert sand.

'What is it?' **they** wondered, looking at each other.

'Go ahead,' said **Moses**. 'Pick it up.' So **they** did. It looked like coriander seed, and when they bit into it, it tasted like crackers covered in honey. **Moses** told them that they were only allowed to collect enough for one day. When **some** of them disobeyed and stored the food overnight, it filled up with maggots and got really **smelly**.

Every morning, **the food** was there for them to collect. **God** took great care of them and **they** never felt hungry.

WHOOSH

A while later, the **people** ran out of water and felt thirsty again. **They** moaned on and on at Moses, but **he** knew that God would look after them, so **he** talked to **God**.

'What am I going to do with them, God?' **he** asked. 'They never stop moaning.'

God told **Moses** to take his stick and hit it against a **rock**. When **he** did, clear **water** gushed out of the **rock** and **everyone** had plenty to drink.

Eventually, **they** came to the foot of a **mountain**, called Sinai. Nobody was allowed to put so much as a single foot on this mountain. **Moses** called all the people together and posted **guards**. While **they** were standing there, a thick **cloud** covered the **mountain** top. **Thunder** cracked and **lightning** crackled. A **trumpet** blew, louder and louder, as **smoke** and **fire** poured out of the cloud.

WHOOSH

God told **Moses** that he wanted to give the people rules to live by, and Moses needed to climb the mountain to talk to God about them. So, leaving his brother **Aaron** in charge, **Moses** set off. But **he** was gone for 40 days, and the people started moaning—again.

'What's the point in having a God you can't see?' **they** complained to **Aaron**.

So **Aaron** collected all of their gold and made it into a **golden calf**. When **Moses** eventually returned, **he** found the **people** dancing around the **statue**, having a huge party. **He** was so angry with them that **he** smashed the **golden statue** to pieces.

The people were very sad about what they had done. **They** told **God** that they were sorry and

promised to obey God and keep the rules that he had given to Moses. That way, **they** would show that they were God's people.

WHOOSH

Follow up

Discussion

- What does it mean to trust someone?
- Whom do we trust (family, friends, and so on)?
- Why do we trust them?
- In this story, people didn't trust God when they were hungry and thirsty. What did God do to care for them every time they needed something?
- Did they learn to trust God?

Activity

- Fill an unmarked box with shredded paper. Inside it, hide enough treats for everyone. Explain that you are going to ask each person in turn to put their hand in the box and take out a treat. Children must trust you for two things—first, that there is actually something in the box for everyone, and second, that the box contains good things, not bad.
- End by discussing how trust has worked in this activity.

Prayer

Father, thank you that you care for me. Please help me to understand what it means to trust you and not to worry. Amen

13

Joshua: a new leader

NUMBERS 13:1—14:9; JOSHUA 1—2

characters	objects	sounds
Israelite people God Moses twelve spies people Caleb Joshua two spies king of Jericho Rahab messenger guards	new country cities plants Jericho hills window	complaining and moaning banging on a door

The **Israelite people** had travelled across the desert for many years, to a **new country** that God had promised to give them. As they got near to it, **God** told **Moses** that the country called Canaan was to be their new home, but, first, they needed to know what it was like. So **God** told **Moses** to choose **twelve men** to go exploring. **Moses** wanted to know who lived there, what kind of towns they lived in, whether plants and trees grew well in the soil, and whether it was a good land.

So off went the **twelve spies**. **They** spent 40 days travelling around, looking at **cities**, watching **people** and **eating** the luscious fruit that grew all around them. There was plenty of everything—milk to drink and honey to eat. To prove how good the fruit was, **they** cut a single branch of grapes. The branch was so heavy that **they** had to hang it on a pole, and **two men** were needed to carry it. When **they** had collected some pomegranates and some figs, they went back to **Moses**.

WHOOSH

When **they** got back, everyone crowded round, wanting to know what they had found and what their new home would be like. **The spies** described a rich land where the soil was good and the **plants** grew well. **They** showed the fruit they had brought back. **Everyone** got very excited as they chattered to each other.

But then, **some** of the spies started talking about the cities.

'They're huge, with big, strong walls around them,' one **man** said.

'And you should see the people—they're giants,' **another** said. 'We just looked like little grasshoppers.'

The mood quickly changed as **people** started to moan at **Moses**.

'Why didn't we just stay in Egypt?' **they** complained. 'If only we'd died in the desert.'

'Let's choose a leader to take us back to Egypt,' **someone** said, as **everyone** started to **complain** and **moan** at the same time. **Some** even started to cry.

'Stop!' shouted **Caleb**, one of the spies.

'God is with us. Don't be afraid,' encouraged **Joshua**, another of the spies.

WHOOSH

Eventually the **people** did stop grumbling and **they** even **felt** sorry for doubting God. He had always looked after them in the past. By this time, **Moses** was an old man, and one day **he** called all the people together to tell them that **Joshua** was going to be their new leader. Not long afterwards, **Moses** died. **Everyone** was very sad, but **they** promised to follow **Joshua** and obey him, just as they had followed Moses. Soon it was time to get ready to go to their new home.

'Be strong,' said **Joshua**. 'Be brave. God is with us.'

Joshua wanted to know even more about the place where they were going, especially a city called **Jericho**, so **he** decided to send **two spies** ahead of him, to see what they could find out.

WHOOSH

The **two men** set out in secret, but somehow the **king** of Jericho got to hear that there were Israelite spies in his city. **They** were staying with a woman called **Rahab**, and a **messenger** soon arrived from the king, telling her to hand over the spies who were in her house.

Quickly **they** climbed on to the roof and **she** covered them up with piles of plant stalks that were drying in the sun. When the **guards** came **banging** on the door, **she** said she had no idea where the men were, although she thought **she** had seen them leaving the city earlier.

Rahab was very frightened. **She** went up on to the roof to talk to the spies.

'We know that God has given you this land,' **she** said. 'We're all terrified.'

Because **Rahab** had hidden them when the **guards** came, **the spies** promised that they would take care of her and her family when God gave them the land.

WHOOSH

The **spies** had to get away before the guards realised they had been tricked and came back to find them. So **Rahab** let them down to the ground by a rope and told them to hide in the **hills** for a while until the **guards** had stopped searching. After they left, **she** got some scarlet cord and tied it in her **window**, so that, when the spies came back, they would keep her and her family safe.

After hiding for a while, the **spies** returned to **Joshua**.

'God will give us the country,' **they** told him. 'The people who live there are terrified of us.'

So **Joshua** called **everyone** together and got ready to leave for Canaan—their new home, the home that God had promised them when they left Egypt.

WHOOSH

Follow up

Discussion

- Why did the people moan and complain so much?
- What were they frightened of?
- Compare giants with God. What might the giants in Canaan do? What had God done for the Israelite people? Did they need to be afraid?
- When they heard about the giants and the strong cities, the people were overcome with fear. What did Joshua say to them? What had they forgotten about God?

Activity

- Make a pair of spy binoculars.
- Decorate two cardboard tubes and glue them together. Make a hole in the side of each tube and thread with string.
- On one tube write, 'Be bold'. On the other tube write, 'Be brave'. On the reverse side write, 'God is with us'.

Prayer

Father, thank you for this story. Thank you for helping me to understand how much you love and care for us, even when we grumble and complain. Help me as I learn to trust you. Amen

14

Joshua and the walls of Jericho

JOSHUA 3:14–24; 5:10—6:27

characters	objects	sounds
God	River Jordan	people chatting
Israelite people	cattle	slamming windows
Joshua	gold chest	creaking gates
children	heap of water	trumpets blaring
priests	altar	people shouting
twelve men	Jericho's city walls	
people inside Jericho	gates	
seven priests		
armed guards		

God had led the **Israelite people** out of slavery in Egypt to a new home in a land called Canaan. **They** were all camped near the **River Jordan**, waiting for their leader Joshua to tell them when it was time to go. Their **chatter** and **noise** drifted towards the river.

Finally **he** gave the command. **Everyone** started to pack their tents, round up their **cattle** and make sure that their **children** were together. The first people to leave were the **priests**, carrying a beautiful **gold chest**. God had given their leader Moses some rules that they were to live by and the rules were written on pieces of stone. The **gold chest** was very, very special because it was where they stored the stones.

It was spring, and as they came to the edge of the **river**, they could see that it was **flooding**. But as soon as the **priests** stepped into the water, the **river** stopped flowing. All the **water** upstream piled up in a **great big heap** and the **people** just walked across the river bed into Canaan, their new country. **They** were amazed to see that their feet stayed completely dry.

WHOOSH

When **everyone** had walked across, **Joshua** told **twelve men** to collect a huge rock each from the river bed. **They** used the rocks to build an **altar** on the edge of the river bank. It would remind their people for ever that God had given them this country.

When that was done, **Joshua** told the **priests** to finish walking across the river bed and join everyone else. When **they** were safely in Canaan, the **river** started flooding again, just as if nothing had happened. **Everyone** unpacked their tents and set up camp. While they were in the desert, they had eaten manna, a special food that God had provided for them each morning. But today, for the first time in 40 years, **they** ate bread, roasted grain and crops that had been grown in their new country. God had kept his promise. He had given them their own home.

As **they** looked out from their camp, they could see the **people** of **Jericho** shutting up the city tightly. All the windows were slammed shut. All the **gates** creaked closed. Nobody went in or out of the **city**, because they were so afraid of the Israelites and their God.

WHOOSH

Joshua was looking at the big, strong **walls** of Jericho, wondering what to do next.

'Don't worry,' **God** said. 'Jericho already belongs to you. This is what I want you to do.'

Joshua listened to God, then **he** called everyone together.

'Get the gold chest,' he told the **priests**.

'Get a trumpet each,' he told **seven** of the priests.

'Line up in front of the chest,' he told the **armed guards**.

Then **he** lined all the **people** up behind this group and **told** them to walk all around the outside of the **city** in silence. 'Not a single word. Not a sound,' **he** told them. 'Not until I say so.' The **trumpets** blared out all the time they were walking.

And that was it. **They** all went back to their camp and went to bed.

WHOOSH

The next morning, **Joshua** got **everyone** up very early. **He** told the priests to fetch the **gold chest**. He told **seven** of the priests to get a trumpet each. **He** told the **armed guard** to walk ahead of the **chest** and **everyone** else to walk behind it. Off **they** went again, **walking** once around the **city walls** in complete silence. Then **they** went back to their camp.

Each day, for another **four days, they** lined up in exactly the same way—**guards, seven priests** with a trumpet each, **priests** carrying the **gold chest**, and then all the **people. Everyone** inside the city wondered what was going on as **they** looked out. This didn't look like an army. This didn't look like an invasion. Why were these people walking around their city in silence, with their priests sounding trumpets? They didn't have to wait long to find out!

WHOOSH

On the seventh day, **everyone** lined up again, just as they had on the previous six days. But this time was different: this time, instead of walking around the city once, **they** walked around it seven times without stopping. On the seventh time, the **priests** sounded the **trumpets**, and finally, after six days of silence, **Joshua** told the **people** to shout. When all the **people** shouted, the **city walls** fell down with a mighty rumble.

'The city belongs to God!' **Joshua** shouted. **Everyone** rushed into the city. God had promised to give them a new home. They needn't have been afraid. God had kept his promise. They could trust him to take care of them.

WHOOSH

Follow up

Discussion

- What was the problem with Joshua and the people wanting to go into Jericho?
- How did God solve the problem?
- What did the people have to do, in order to go into the city?
- How many different examples can you find in this Whoosh of the people learning to trust and obey God?

Activity

- Decorate a sheet of thin A4 card on one side and roll it into a trumpet shape, decorated side outwards. Tape the edge.
- Practise some trumpet blasts. Then go outside, walk around the building and blow on the trumpets. Why doesn't the building fall down?

Prayer

Thank you, Father, that there are stories in the Bible that help us understand what it means to trust and obey you. Help me to trust you this week. Amen

15

Gideon leads God's people

JUDGES 6—7

characters	objects	sounds
people God Midianites Gideon angel servants	country animals camels cattle sheep caves tree altar to Baal altar to God bull sheep's fleece bowl ground river tent hills	trumpets blasting jars smashing shouting

After many years as slaves in Egypt, the Israelite **people** were given their own **country**. **God** also gave them rules, so that their country would be a fair and safe place to live and everyone would know that they were God's people. Sadly, once **they** settled in their new country, **they** forgot all about God; **they** stopped keeping his rules and **worshipped** other gods.

People from Midian started raiding their land. Every time **the Israelites** planted their fields, the **Midianites** would ride in and let their **camels** eat the growing crops. Then **they** would steal food, **cattle** and **sheep**. Eventually, the **Israelites** had nothing left. **They** were so hungry and frightened that **they** started living in **caves** high up in the mountains. **They** called out to God to help them.

WHOOSH

One day, **Gideon** was threshing grain when an **angel** appeared and sat down under a big **tree** nearby. 'God is with you,' the **angel** said.

Gideon frowned: he knew all the stories about their great leaders, Moses and Joshua. He knew how they had been rescued from slavery in Egypt.

'Where is God now, then?' **he** asked.

'Be strong, Gideon,' the **angel** answered. 'God wants you to save the people.'

'Me?' **he** laughed. 'I'm not important. I can't do that.'

'You can,' said the **angel**, 'because God is with you.'

Then the **angel** disappeared. **Gideon** built an **altar** there, so that people could worship God.

WHOOSH

That night, **God** spoke to **Gideon** again. **He** told **him** to go and pull down an **altar** to Baal, a god that Gideon's father and lots of other people worshipped. So off went **Gideon** with some of his **servants**. First they killed a **bull** that his father owned. Then, while it was still dark and nobody could see them, they pulled the **altar** down. Finally, they built an **altar** to God, using stones, and they burnt the **bull** as an offering.

The next morning, **everyone** was really angry when they saw that the altar to Baal had gone and had been replaced with one to the true God.

WHOOSH

They soon forgot about it, though, when the **Midianites** invaded again. This time, thousands of them **set up** camp in the Israelites' fields. **Gideon** knew that it was time to act. **He** called everyone together to make an army to defeat the Midianites once and for all.

But **Gideon** kept thinking about what the angel had said. **He** needed to know if God really wanted him to save the people, so **he** asked God for a sign. He put a **sheep's fleece** on the floor. **He** asked God to make the fleece wet but keep the ground dry. Sure enough, when **he** got up next morning, the **fleece** was wet. He wrung a **bowlful** of water out of it, although the **ground** was completely dry.

'Please don't be angry with me, God,' **he** prayed, 'but could you just do it the other way round tomorrow?' And **God** did just that: the next morning, the **fleece** was dry and the **ground** was wet.

WHOOSH

Gideon was ready. **He** looked around at the huge army. Surely 30,000 men would beat the Midianites, **he** thought.

'The army is too big,' said **God**. 'I want everyone to understand that I am winning this battle, not them.'

So **Gideon** told everyone who was frightened to go home. More than **half the army** disappeared.

'It's still too big,' said **God**. He told **Gideon** to take **them** to the **river** and watch how **they** drank. **Most** of them knelt with their faces near the water. Just 300 **men** scooped water up in their hands, so that **they** could keep watch.

'Take just those 300 men,' said **God**. 'You will win.'

WHOOSH

God knew that **Gideon** was still frightened, so **he** told Gideon to take a **servant** and go to the enemy camp. As **Gideon** knelt near a **tent**, **he** heard the men inside talking.

'God is going to give our camp to Gideon,' **one of them** said. So even their enemies knew they were going to win! **Gideon** worshipped God as he returned to the Israelite camp to get ready. **He** told every man to **take** a trumpet and to put a torch inside an empty jar. Then, in the middle of the night, **they** completely encircled the **Midianites**. At a sign from **Gideon**, the **men** blew their trumpets, **smashed** their jars and **held** the torches up high. 'For God and for Gideon!' **they** shouted, sounding like a great army.

Woken suddenly, the **Midianites** were so terrified that **they** started killing each other. **Those** who escaped ran off into the **hills**, pursued by the **Israelite** army.

As the **people** celebrated, **they** were sorry that they had disobeyed God. **They** promised to live as his people in the land that he had given them.

WHOOSH

Follow up

Discussion

- Think of some people who are important. What makes them important?
- Gideon felt unimportant but God wanted him to be a leader. Why did God choose him?
- Why did God want only 300 men in the army?
- Do we need to be important before we can do things for God?

Activity

- Decorate a long tube, such as the inside of a paper towel roll, in flame colours. Write on the tube, 'Go in the strength you have' (Judges 6:14, NIV), to remind children that God can use us, however unimportant we are.
- Use flame-coloured cellophane, card or tissue paper to make flames. Glue them to the inside of the tube to represent a flaming torch.

Prayer

Thank you, God, that I don't need to be important before I can do things for you. Thank you that you accept me just as I am. Amen

16

Samson the strong man

JUDGES 13:1—16:31

characters	objects	sounds
people of Israel	fire	buzzing bees
Philistines	Samson's home	shouting Philistines
Manoah and his wife	Philistine woman's home	cracking pillars
angel	Delilah's house	crashing building
Samson	vineyards	
Philistine woman	lion	
her parents	bees	
party guests	skeleton	
Delilah	party	
Philistine rulers	camp	
	cave	
	prison	
	feast	
	two pillars	

Once again, as they had done many times before, the **people** of Israel forgot about God. **They** stopped keeping his rules and **they** stopped worshipping him. So God allowed the **Philistines** to invade their country.

One day, **Manoah** and his **wife** were visited by an **angel**. **They** were puzzled, because **they** didn't realise who it was. The **angel** told them that they were going to have a baby, a special boy. His hair must never be cut, as a sign that he belonged to God. **Manoah** built a **fire** on top of a large rock as an altar to God, but as **they** watched, the **fire** blazed up towards the sky and the **angel** went up into the sky inside the flames. Suddenly **they** realised that the visitor was an angel from God.

WHOOSH

Samson grew into a fine, strong young man. One day, he met a **Philistine woman**. **He** went straight **home** to tell his **parents** that this was the woman he wanted to marry. **They** were upset because the Philistines didn't worship God. **They** tried to persuade him to marry an Israelite girl, but **he** was determined.

So they set off to her **home** to visit her **parents**. On the way, as **they** passed some **vineyards**, a young **lion** sprang towards **Samson**, but **he** was so strong that he killed it. The next time **he** was out walking that way, **he** stopped to look at the dead lion. **He** was amazed to see that **bees** had started living in the **skeleton**. **He** scooped out some of the sweet honey and ate it.

Soon it was time for the wedding. **Samson** threw a huge **party** that lasted for seven days. **He** bet the other **men** there that if they could solve a riddle by the end of the party, **he** would buy them all new clothes. If they couldn't solve it, they would each have to buy him some new clothes. And this was the riddle:

'Out of the eater, something to eat.

Out of the strong, something sweet.'

They scratched their heads for days, and **they** nagged at Samson's **girlfriend** to make **Samson** tell her the answer.

WHOOSH

'You don't really love me,' **she** cried and whinged, until eventually **Samson** explained the riddle. Honey had come out of the skeleton of the dead lion. **She** rushed off and told her **friends**, so Samson lost the bet. **He** was so angry that he stormed out of the party. Later, **he** set fire to the Philistine wheatfields, just to get his own back. And so a terrible conflict began.

The **Philistines** set up a huge army **camp** to try to catch Samson. His own **people** were so frightened that **they** themselves went to get Samson from the **cave** where he was living and hand him over to the Philistines.

'Why did you provoke our enemies?' **they** asked.

'They started it,' shrugged **Samson** as they tied him up.

Thinking they had won, the **Philistine** soldiers started **shouting** as they ran towards him, but just as his own **people** were about to hand him over, **Samson** stretched himself and **snapped** the ropes. Then, **picking** up a jawbone from a donkey's skeleton, **he** killed a thousand Philistines before escaping.

WHOOSH

Then, one day, **Samson** fell in love with **Delilah**. The **Philistine rulers** saw their chance and offered her eleven hundred silver pieces if she could help them trap Samson.

'Samson,' **she** asked one day when he was at her **house**, 'what makes you so strong?'

He told her to tie him up with seven new bowstrings and he would lose his strength. **She** did, but when the **Philistines** came rushing in, **he** just broke the strings.

'Why did you make me look stupid?' **she** asked. 'Tell me the truth.'

This time, **he** told her to use new ropes, but **he** broke those, too. Then **he** told her to weave his hair into the cloth on her loom, but **he** broke free when the Philistines arrived.

Finally, worn out by **her** constant nagging, **he** told her the truth. The next time **he** fell asleep, **she** cut off all his hair. When the **Philistines** arrived this time, **he** couldn't break free.

WHOOSH

Samson was thrown into **prison**. **He** was only allowed out to push round a huge, heavy millstone to grind grain. One day, the **Philistines** were having a **feast**. **They** were all having a good time and **they** called for Samson to be brought to amuse them. When **he** was led out, he stood between two **pillars**. What the Philistines hadn't realised, though, was that while he was in prison, his hair had grown long again.

Reaching out to the pillars, **Samson** pushed and pushed until, with a mighty crack, the **pillars** crumbled. Thousands of **Philistines**, together with **Samson**, died as the temple crashed to the ground.

WHOOSH

Follow up

Discussion

- Why could Samson never cut his hair?
- Why was Delilah tempted to trick Samson?
- How did Samson use his gift of strength to help God and his people?
- How can we use our gifts to help God and other people?

Activity

- Give each child a potato with the top cut off and some of the pulp scooped out.
- Draw a face on the potato and write, 'Be strong in the Lord' on the back of the potato. Sprinkle cress seeds into the open top.
- Keep the seeds watered and watch the hair grow on the potato head.

Prayer

Father God, I know that you have given me a special gift. Help me to use it for you and to help other people, too. Amen

17

Ruth chooses a family

RUTH 1—4

characters	objects	sounds
Naomi	rain	
Elimelech	crops	
Mahlon	Moab	
Kilion	Bethlehem	
Orpah	road	
Ruth	shelter	
people	water jars	
men harvesting	stalks	
Boaz	sheaves	
foreman	home	
cousin	grain store	
ten elders	town gate	
Obed		

Naomi and **Elimelech** were very hungry. No **rain** fell, the **crops** died, and nobody had enough food to eat. As **they** watched their two sons, **Mahlon** and **Kilion**, get hungrier and hungrier, they decided to move to **Moab** until there was rain in Israel.

They settled down in their new country, and **Elimelech** worked hard, growing enough **crops** to feed his family. Then, one day, something terrible happened. **Elimelech** died. **Naomi** was left alone with her **two sons**. For a while, it seemed that life would be OK. **Mahlon** and **Kilion** married local girls **Orpah** and **Ruth**, and they were a happy family again. But then tragedy struck for a second time. **Mahlon** and **Kilion** also died, leaving **Naomi, Orpah** and **Ruth** all alone.

WHOOSH

One day, **Naomi** heard that the famine in Israel had ended and that **people** had enough to eat again. **She** decided to go back home to **Bethlehem**. Off she set with **Orpah** and **Ruth**, but they hadn't gone far along the **road** when **Naomi** stopped and looked sadly at the two young women.

'Go back home,' **she** urged them. 'You need to be with your own people.' At first, **Orpah** refused, but then **she** changed her mind. Hugging **Naomi, she** turned and walked away in tears.

'Go on, Ruth,' **Naomi** said. 'You go, too.'

But **Ruth** refused to leave Naomi. 'Where you go, I will go,' **she** said. 'Your God will be my God.' No matter how much **Naomi** argued, **Ruth** refused to leave. Eventually, realising how determined Ruth was, **Naomi** turned and walked with her towards Bethlehem.

When **they** arrived, **everyone** was very excited to see **Naomi** again after so many years, and **everyone** wanted to meet **Ruth**.

WHOOSH

Harvest was just beginning. **Ruth** and **Naomi** had nothing to eat, so Ruth decided to go out into the fields and pick up any grain that had fallen while the **crops** were being harvested. **Naomi** waved her off, and soon **Ruth** was following behind the **men** harvesting the barley, **picking** up any bits that they dropped. **She** worked hard all morning, only stopping once for a rest in the **shelter**.

While they were working, **Boaz**, the owner of the field, arrived.

'Who is that young woman over there?' **he** asked the **foreman**.

'Ruth, the girl who came back from Moab with Naomi,' **he** answered. 'She asked if she could pick up any dropped grain.'

Boaz went over to **Ruth**.

'In future,' **he** said, 'make sure you only collect grain in *my* fields. And when you're thirsty, help yourself to water from the **water jars**.'

'Thank you,' said **Ruth** as she bowed to **Boaz**. 'But why are you helping me?'

Boaz explained that he had heard how kind she had been to Naomi. At lunch time, **he** offered her food to eat, and before he left **he** told his **men** to **pull** some **stalks** from the **sheaves** deliberately and drop them for her.

So **Ruth** worked hard until the evening, and **she** collected a lot of grain.

WHOOSH

Naomi was pleased when **Ruth** arrived **home** with all the grain and told her what had happened. When **Naomi** asked who the kind man was, **Ruth** answered, 'Boaz.' Then **Naomi** got really excited. 'He's a relative of ours,' she said. 'He will take care of us.'

So every day, **Ruth** would follow along behind the **harvesters**, collecting any grain that fell. When the barley harvest ended, **she** did the same again, every day, right through the wheat harvest. **She** and **Naomi** had plenty of grain to **grind** into flour and then to **make** into bread.

One day, **Naomi** decided that it was time for Ruth to think about marrying again. So when the wheat harvest was finished, **she** told **Ruth** to put on her best clothes and nicest perfume and go to the **grain store** where **Boaz** was working.

'God will bless you,' **he** said when **she** arrived, 'for all the kindness that you have shown Naomi.' Then **he** took her shawl and filled it with grain to take home to Naomi.

'I'll take care of you,' **he** promised as she left.

WHOOSH

Next morning, **Boaz** sat down at the **town gate** and waited until a **cousin** of his passed by. Then he called ten of the town's **elders** to join him and said to his **cousin**, 'One of us must buy Naomi's land and marry Ruth.' But the **cousin** didn't want to marry her, so **Boaz** agreed with the town's **elders** that he would marry Ruth himself.

So **Boaz** bought Elimelech's land from **Naomi** and **married Ruth**. When their son **Obed** was born, **Naomi** cuddled him and cared for him. **Everyone** smiled when they saw **her** with her grandson. What they couldn't possibly know, as **they** watched **Obed** grow up, was that Obed's grandson David would be the greatest king Israel ever had.

WHOOSH

Follow up

Discussion

- Why do you think Ruth went with Naomi rather than going back home to her own people?
- What promise did Ruth make to Naomi?
- How did God take care of them?
- Why was Boaz so kind to them?

Activity

- Roll a piece of thick paper into a tube and secure the edges with tape.
- Make four cuts vertically at one end of the roll. Pull the inner sections of the roll upwards, though not far enough to allow the individual strands of paper to curl over.
- Cut teardrop shapes (representing individual grains of wheat) from light brown paper and stick them to the strands of paper at the end of the tube.
- Why were individual stalks of wheat important in Ruth's story?

Prayer

Father, please help me to show the sort of courage that Ruth showed when she was so kind to Naomi. Help me to be a good friend, just as Ruth was. Amen

18

Hannah's baby

1 SAMUEL 1—3

characters	objects	sounds
Elkanah	temple	voice of God
Hannah	feast	
friends	temple door	
children	home	
Eli	temple light	
Samuel		
people		
three brothers		
two sisters		
two sons of Eli		
servants		

Elkanah loved his wife **Hannah** very much and he was very kind, but, even so, **Hannah** was sad. **Hannah** and **Elkanah** both loved God, so every year they would **go** on a journey to the **temple** at Shiloh, to worship God and **go** to a **feast** with their **friends**. That was when **Hannah** was most sad, because their **friends** all had **children** and she had none. Sometimes other **people** even teased her about it and showed off because they had children. **Elkanah** felt sorry for **Hannah**, and, when **he** was serving food at the feast, **he** often gave her extra because **he** wanted to show her that **he** loved her so much.

Once, when **they** were all at a **feast, Hannah** was so upset that **she** couldn't eat anything. **Choking** back her tears until she was on her own, **she** left her friends and went into the **temple**, where it was quiet. **Eli**, the priest, was **sitting** by the **door**. There in the temple, **Hannah** prayed and told God all about her pain and her sadness because she had no children. She promised that if she had a son, she would give him back to God. As **she** prayed, her **lips** moved soundlessly.

Watching her from his seat by the **temple door, Eli** thought she was drunk from having too much wine at the feast. But when **he** went over to her and **she** told him what was wrong, **he** said, 'God will hear your prayers.'

The next morning, **Hannah** and **Elkanah** set out for **home**.

WHOOSH

God did hear Hannah's prayers and **Elkanah** and **Hannah** had a **baby boy**. They called him Samuel. That year, when it was time to visit the **temple** for the feast, **Hannah** decided to stay at **home** because Samuel was so tiny. But **she** told **Elkanah** about the promise she had made to God, and **she** knew that, when he was older, she would take Samuel to the temple and leave him there to serve God.

Sure enough, a few years later, when **they** went with their friends to the annual feast, **Elkanah** and **Hannah** took **Samuel** to **Eli** the priest, saying, 'We give him to the Lord.' Before **they** left to go **home, Hannah** prayed again. But this time her prayer was full of joy because God had given her a son.

WHOOSH

Every morning, **Samuel** had the job of opening the big **temple doors** so that **people** could come into the temple to pray. Then **he** would help with all the jobs that needed doing. Every year, when his **parents** visited for the **feast, Hannah** would bring some new clothes for him. **She** watched him grow and learn to love God, and, as the years passed, his **three brothers** and **two sisters** would come to the temple **feast**, too.

WHOOSH

Eli the priest had **two sons** who were also priests. **They** had grown up to be very bad men. When **people** brought animals to the **temple** to make sacrifices to God, **they** would always give some of the meat to the **priest** after the sacrifice had been made. But Eli's **sons** wouldn't wait for the sacrifices to be made. Instead, they would send their **servants** to take away the meat immediately. **People** were getting really cross with Eli's **sons**, but, although **Eli** warned them that they were making God angry, **they** just ignored him and kept on taking what they wanted from **people. They** didn't listen to **Eli**, and eventually even **Eli** stopped listening to God. **Samuel**, though, was learning to love God. As **Eli** became old and nearly blind, **he** relied more and more on **Samuel** for help.

WHOOSH

One night, **Samuel** was lying in his bed in the **temple**, watching the **light** burn out, when he heard a **voice** calling, 'Samuel.'

He got up and **went** to **Eli's** room to ask him what he wanted.

'I didn't call,' **Eli** said. 'Go back to bed.'

It happened again.

'Samuel,' the **voice** called. Again, **Samuel** went to **Eli**.

'It wasn't me. Go back to bed,' muttered **Eli**.

A third time, **Samuel** heard his name called. This time when he went to **Eli, Eli** realised that it was God calling Samuel.

'Go back to bed,' said **Eli**, 'and next time he calls, say, "Speak to me, God. I'm listening."'

So back **Samuel** went to bed, and the next time **he** heard a voice saying, 'Samuel, Samuel,' **he** did as Eli said. He answered, 'Speak to me, God. I'm listening.'

WHOOSH

The next morning, **Samuel** opened the heavy **temple doors** as usual. **He** heard **Eli** calling to him, asking what God had said. At first, **Samuel** didn't want to tell him, but **Eli** insisted.

So **Samuel** told him everything—that because Eli's **sons** were so wicked and **Eli** hadn't done anything about it, his family couldn't carry on being priests any more.

As **Samuel** grew up, **people** who came to the **temple** to worship saw that **he** loved God and that one day he would make a great leader of their people.

WHOOSH

Follow up

Discussion

- Why did Hannah promise to give Samuel back to God?
- How did God bless her for choosing to do this?
- What happened when Eli stopped listening to God?
- Why did people respect Samuel?

Activity

- Use card to cut out two large ears, one left and one right. On one ear write, 'Speak to me, God.' On the other ear write, 'I'm listening.'
- Fold a long pipe cleaner to make a headband. Tape an ear on to each end of the pipe cleaner to make a head bopper.

Prayer

Thank you, Father God, that you listen to my prayers. Help me always to be ready to listen to your answers. Amen

19

David fights a giant

1 SAMUEL 16:1—17:58

characters	objects	sounds
people of Israel	Bethlehem	shrieking
Samuel	Samuel's home	shouting
God	army camp	
Saul	sheep	
Jesse	tent	
eight sons	lions	
David	bears	
army	stream	
army commanders		
Philistine army		
Goliath		

The **people of Israel** badly wanted a king, just like the other countries around them had. When **Samuel** told **God** how the people felt, **God** said, 'I'm their king.' But eventually **they** moaned about it to **Samuel** so much that **God** agreed to let them have a king, even though he knew that it would mean trouble.

Their first king was **Saul**. **Samuel** poured special oil on his head to show that he was the king, and for a while **he** trusted God and led the people well. But then **he** started disobeying God. **God** was sorry that he had chosen Saul as king, and, for a long time, **Samuel** was very sad. Eventually, **God** told **Samuel** that he had been feeling miserable for long enough: it was time to choose a new king to take over when Saul died.

So off went **Samuel** to **Bethlehem**, looking for a man called **Jesse** who had **eight sons**.

WHOOSH

Jesse's eldest son, **Eliab**, was a tall, strong soldier in Saul's army. **He** already looked like a king as **he** walked into the room.

'This must be the one,' **Samuel** thought. But **God** said, 'No,' because although **Eliab** looked good on the outside, **his** heart didn't belong to God. And so it went on, **son** after **son**, until **Samuel** had met **seven** of them. Each time, **Samuel** thought this son must be the one God wanted to be the next king. Each time, **God** said, 'No.'

'Is that it?' **he** asked **Jesse** after he had met **seven** of his sons.

'No. There's one more, the youngest. But he's just a shepherd,' answered **Jesse**.

Samuel asked for **David** to be brought to him, and, as **David** appeared, **God** said to **Samuel**, 'This is the one.' So, although David was still very young, **Samuel** poured oil on his head to show that he was going to be the next king. Then **Samuel** left **Bethlehem** and went **home**.

WHOOSH

As well as being a shepherd, **David** was a good musician. Sometimes King **Saul** would get really miserable, and **David**'s harp playing would cheer him up. In fact, it cheered him up so much that **he** sent a message to **Jesse** saying that **David** would be staying with him.

So there was **David**, **going** backwards and forwards between Saul's **army camp** and his father's **sheep**. Sometimes **he** played his harp for the **king** in his **tent**, and sometimes he cared for the **sheep** in his father's fields. With wild animals around, being a shepherd could be dangerous and **David** sometimes had to use a slingshot to kill the **lions** and **bears** that tried to attack the **sheep**. He was a good shot, though. No wild animals harmed *his* sheep.

WHOOSH

David's three oldest **brothers** were already soldiers in King Saul's **army**. One day, **Jesse** told **David** to leave the **sheep** and **take** some food to his **brothers** and to the **army commanders**. He told **David** that he was to come back and tell him how his brothers were getting on. But when **David** got to the **camp**, **he** found all the **soldiers** already lined up for battle with the **Philistines**. Suddenly, **they** all started looking really scared.

'What's happening?' **David** asked one of the **soldiers**. The **soldier** pointed to the hugest **giant** that David had ever seen. **He** was almost as tall as two ordinary people. Every morning and evening for 40 days, **Goliath** the giant had appeared, **waving** his spear and **roaring** at the Israelites, daring them to send a man to fight him. **Everyone** was terrified of him—everyone except **David**.

David rushed back to Saul's **tent**.

'I'll fight him,' **David** said. 'God will help me.'

Saul wasn't sure at first, but **David** got impatient and **insisted** that if he could kill lions and bears, **he** could certainly kill a giant. So **Saul** agreed. **He** gave **David** his armour and his weapons, but they were far too big and heavy for David. After **wobbling** around in it a bit, **he** gave it all back. **Leaving** the **tent**, **he** picked up five small, smooth stones from a **stream** and walked to the front line of the **soldiers**.

WHOOSH

'What?' roared **Goliath** when he spotted **David**. 'A little boy!' **he** laughed.

'You come at me with a sword,' said **David** calmly. 'But I come at you in the name of God.' **He** took one of the stones, **put** it in his slingshot, **swung** it round and round, and then **let go**. The stone hit **Goliath** right on the forehead.

The **Philistines** were so frightened when they saw their **hero** fall down dead that **they** ran away, **shrieking** in terror. The Israelite **army** pursued them, **shouting** at the tops of their voices.

And so the **Philistines** were driven out of their land.

WHOOSH

Follow up

Discussion

- Jesse's oldest son was a strong, brave soldier. Why didn't God choose him as the next king?
- Why did God choose David?
- What sort of people does God want us to be?
- How can we become those sort of people?

Activity

- Give each pair of children an apple. Talk about what it looks like, what colour skin it has, and so on. How do we know whether the apple is as nice inside as outside? Might there be something bad inside the apple? Or something good?
- Cut each apple in half horizontally. Inside every apple when it's cut this way is a star, which has never been seen before because it can't be seen from the outside. Eat the apple halves.

Prayer

Thank you, Father, that it's what is on the inside of me that matters to you, not what I look like or how other people see me. Help me to grow a heart that loves you. Amen

20
Solomon makes wise choices

1 KINGS 3: 5–7

characters	objects	sounds
Israelite people	palace	
Saul	feast	
David	trees	
Solomon	blocks of stone	
Pharaoh	temple	
Pharaoh's daughter	a room for the special box	
God	carved angels	
two women	carved trees/flower blossoms	
baby	bronze pillars	
servant	gold furniture	
kings and queens		
architects		
work teams		

Although God was their true king, the **Israelite people** wanted a human king, like the other countries around them. Their first king, **Saul**, had stopped following God. But **David**, their next king, had loved God and, although **he** had often made mistakes, **he** had been a great king. **He** lived to be a very old man and, when he died, his son **Solomon** became king in his place.

Solomon knew that **he** needed to follow God and obey him if he was going to be a good king like his father. The first thing **he** did was to make friends with **Pharaoh**, the king of Egypt. **He** even married Pharaoh's **daughter** and built her a **palace** of her own.

But there was one thing that **Solomon** longed to do. As **he** looked out from his **palace** across Jerusalem, he could see **people** at different altars, **praying** to God. **He** wanted to build a temple so that people had a special place where they could go to worship God.

WHOOSH

Sometimes **Solomon** would make a journey to Gibeon, a place where he could worship God. While **he** was there one night, **Solomon** had a dream. He saw **God** standing next to him, saying, 'What do you want? I will give you anything you ask.' In his dream **Solomon** could see his father **David** and **he** thought about what had made him a great king. **He** imagined all the **people** over whom he ruled—too many people to count. Then **he** said to **God**, 'Give me a wise heart so that I will lead your people well.'

God was pleased with Solomon's request. The next day, **Solomon** held a huge **feast** for **everyone** in his royal court, to say 'thank you' to God for giving him wisdom.

WHOOSH

One day, **Solomon** was sitting in his **palace** when **two women** came in, carrying a **baby**. **They** stood in front of him, **scowling** at each other and looking as though a violent argument was going to break out at any minute. Apparently, **they** both thought the baby belonged to them.

'He's mine,' **said** the first woman.

'No he's not, he's mine,' **said** the second woman. 'Your baby died.'

And so **it** went on, back and forth in front of the king.

'Bring me a sword,' called **Solomon** above the argument. Then, as a **servant** came forward with a sword, he said, 'Cut the baby in half and give them half each.'

'No, please don't kill him,' **pleaded** one of the women.

'Why not?' **said** the other woman. 'That way, neither of us will have a baby.'

Solomon told his **servant** to give the **baby** to the **woman** who had pleaded with him not to kill him. She was the real mother.

When **everyone** heard about it, they knew that Solomon was a kind and wise king.

WHOOSH

Solomon ruled over a huge, peaceful kingdom, and **everyone** who lived in it was happy and had plenty to eat. **He** was richer than anyone could imagine; because **he** had asked for wisdom to rule his people, rather than money or fame, God had blessed him with great riches. **Solomon** became famous anyway, for his wisdom: **kings** and **queens** from other countries would come to meet him. **People** would often sit and listen while he talked, because he was so wise.

But **Solomon** kept thinking about the **temple** that he wanted to build for his people to pray in, so his **architects** prepared the plans. **Thousands** of men from all over Israel came to help and Solomon divided them into **teams**. **Some** went to other countries to chop down **trees** and prepare the wood. **Some** cut huge **blocks of stone** ready for building the walls. **Others** moved the **blocks** and the **wood** to Jerusalem. Each **team** would **work** for two months, then they would **go home** to rest for a month while other teams took over.

WHOOSH

And so it was, four years after he became king and more than 400 years after the people of Israel had prepared a special golden box in which they stored the rules that God had given them to live by, that **Solomon** started to build the temple, somewhere for people to worship God.

It was huge, with a **special room** for the box. Everywhere **people** looked, there was pure, dazzling gold—on the walls, on the ceiling and even on the floor. Huge **angels** were carved and then covered in gold. **Trees** and **flower blossoms** were carved in wood, then covered in gold before being used to **decorate** the walls. Huge bronze **pillars** supported the entrance porch, and rich **gold furniture** filled the temple.

For seven years **everyone** was very busy. **People** even came from other countries to help. And then they were done: their magnificent **temple** was finished. **Solomon** had given his people a place to worship God.

Solomon ruled his country peacefully for 40 years. **People** travelled from all over the world to meet him, and **he** became the richest, wisest king on earth.

WHOOSH

Follow up

Discussion

- Why was God pleased with Solomon's choice?
- Solomon chose to walk with God. How did God bless him and his people?
- Why did Solomon want to build the temple?

Activity

- Prepare trays of paint in different colours. Give each child a long strip of paper, such as wallpaper.
- Place bare feet in the paint, then walk along the paper to create footprints. When the paint is dry, write, 'Be wise. Walk with God' underneath the footprints.

Prayer

Father God, thank you that I can walk with you. Please help me to be wise when I have to make decisions. Amen

21

God cares for Elijah

1 KINGS 16:29—18:4

characters	objects	sounds
Ahab	Baal	
God	temple	
Jezebel	rain	
people	royal palace	
prophets	Cherith Creek	
Elijah	stream	
woman	ravens	
son	town gate	
leaders of other countries	fire	
	bowl	
	oil jar	
	Samaria	
	crops	
	animals	

Ahab was the worst king that Israel ever had. Not only did **he** turn away from **God**, but he married **Jezebel**, a woman who told him to worship a false god called **Baal**. **He** built a **temple** to worship Baal. **He** told his **people** that they had to worship **Baal** instead of **God**. **He** took **land** that didn't belong to him. **He** looked the other way while his **wife** killed **prophets** who taught the **people** about God. **He** even punished his own **people** when they carried on worshipping God. **He** made **God** very angry.

WHOOSH

Elijah was a prophet. One day, **God** told **Elijah** to go to **Ahab** with a message. He wanted Ahab to realise that what he was doing was wrong. Because **Ahab** was worshipping **Baal** instead of him, **God** was going to stop it **raining**. There wasn't even going to be any dew in the mornings—nothing.

So off went **Elijah** to visit **Ahab** in his **royal palace**, wondering what **Ahab** would do when he gave him God's message.

'I am a servant of the living God, the God of Israel,' **said** Elijah. 'God says that it isn't going to rain any more until he says so.'

After **Elijah** had delivered his message, **God** told **him** to **get out** of there quickly and to **go** and hide in **Cherith Creek**. **Elijah** walked down into the deep valley and **sat down** by the **stream**. He was safe there because he was well hidden by the steep sides of the valley. There was plenty of water to **drink** in the stream, and every morning and every evening, **ravens** would bring him bread and meat.

But there was **no rain**, so eventually the **stream** dried up and **Elijah** had no more water. 'Go to Zarephath,' **God** told him. 'There's a lady there who will look after you.'

WHOOSH

So **Elijah** started on another journey. It was hot, and he was relieved when he saw the **town gate** of Zarephath in the distance. As **he** neared the gate, **feeling** very tired and thirsty, **he** saw a **woman** picking up sticks for firewood.

'Please could you bring me some water to drink and some bread to eat?' **he** asked.

The **woman** looked at him sadly. 'There's been no rain,' **she** said. 'We have no food.' **She** explained that she was going to use the firewood to bake one more loaf of bread, then all her flour and oil would be used up. After that, **she** and her **son** would die of starvation.

'Use your flour to make some bread,' **Elijah** told her, 'but bring me some of it. God will take care of you.'

WHOOSH

The **woman** trusted what Elijah had told her. **She** lit a **fire**, **poured** the last drop of her precious oil into the flour, and **kneaded** it together to make dough. Then **she** shaped the loaf, **cooked** it and **took** some of the bread to **Elijah**. The rest **she** shared with her **son**.

'That's it,' **she** thought, still feeing hungry. 'There's nothing else to eat.'

But to her amazement, when **she** looked in the **bowl**, there was more flour there. When **she** looked in her **oil jar**, there was oil there. Every day, **there was just enough** to make a meal for her **son**, **Elijah** and **herself**. So even though there was no sign of rain every morning when **she** looked up into the sky, **she** didn't go hungry.

WHOOSH

One day, the woman's **son** became ill. **He** got worse and worse and eventually he died.

'Why has God done this? What have I done to deserve this?' **she** shouted at **Elijah**.

Elijah picked up the **child, carried** him to his room, **laid** him down on the bed and **knelt** down. Then **Elijah** prayed. **He** asked **God** why he had let this happen to a woman who was caring for him. **He** asked **God** why he had let the boy die. Then **he** pleaded with **God** to bring the **boy** back to life.

God answered Elijah's prayer. The **boy** started to breathe, and soon **Elijah** was able to **take him** back downstairs and **give him** to his mother.

'Now I know that you really are a prophet from God and that what you say about him is true,' **she** said.

WHOOSH

But back in **Samaria**, things were going from bad to worse. There was **no rain**, so there were no **crops**. There was no water, so the **animals** died. **People** were starving. In spite of this, **Jezebel**, the queen, was searching out **prophets** of God and killing them. **She** was determined to find **Elijah** and kill him, too. **She** hated him so much that **she** even made **leaders of other countries** look for him too.

Eventually, after three years, **God** told **Elijah** to go back to **Ahab** with another message: he was going to make it rain at last.

WHOOSH

Follow up

Discussion

- Why did Ahab worship false gods?
- Why didn't he do anything when God's prophets were being killed?
- How and why did God care for Elijah?
- What did the woman at Zarephath learn about God?

Activity

- Give each child a paper bag to make a raven puppet.
- If there is time to allow drying, paint the bag black. Cut out wings from black craft paper and stick them in place, one on each side of the bag. Stick on moving eyes. Cut out a D shape from grey paper, to make a beak, and stick in place.
- Write along the bottom of the bag, 'God cared for Elijah'.

Prayer

Father, just as you fed Elijah and cared for him when he was in danger, thank you that you care for me, too. Help me to be bold and brave for you. Amen

22

Elijah and the prophets of Baal

1 KINGS 18:16–46

characters	objects	sounds
people of Israel King Ahab Obadiah Elijah thin, hungry people God prophets of Baal servant	palace Samaria thin cattle Baal Mount Carmel two dead bulls altar to Baal altar to God trench fire tiny cloud thick black clouds heavy rain	shouting hissing of boiling water crackling of burning wood

Everyone in Israel was starving because there had been no rain for nearly three years. **King Ahab** called for **Obadiah**, who was in charge of his **palace**. 'Go right through the country,' **he** told **Obadiah**. 'Find every spring and every stream and every blade of grass to feed our animals.' **He** told **Obadiah** to go one way, and **he** went the other.

Meanwhile, **Elijah**, God's prophet, was walking back to **Samaria**. **He** had been hiding for a long time because **Ahab** was very angry with him. Even so, **God** had told him that he was to visit **Ahab** with a message. Everywhere **Elijah** looked, there were **thin cattle** and **thin, hungry people**. The land was scorched and dry. **He** wondered if the people were ready to say sorry to God yet, for turning away from him.

It was while he was walking that **Elijah** met **Obadiah**.

'Go and tell Ahab that I have a message for him,' said **Elijah**. 'Tell him I want to meet him.'

'Are you crazy?' questioned **Obadiah**. 'He's been looking everywhere for you. When I tell him you're here, first he'll kill me, then he'll come and kill you.'

But **Obadiah** went anyway and told **Ahab** exactly where he could find **Elijah**.

WHOOSH

Straight away, **Ahab** went to meet **Elijah**.

'So here you are, troublemaker,' **Ahab** said when he found **Elijah**.

'I'm not the troublemaker,' answered **Elijah**. 'You are. You turned the people away from God.'

He told **Ahab** that it was time to make up his mind—**God** or **Baal**? **Ahab** had to choose. **Elijah** told **Ahab** to call together all the **prophets** of Baal and all the **people** of Israel and to meet him on the top of **Mount Carmel. They** were to bring **two dead bulls** with them.

Ahab did as Elijah said. **So** there they all were—**Ahab** the king, **Elijah**, who thought he was the only prophet of God left alive, **950 prophets** of Baal, and all the **people** of Israel.

'Choose,' said **Elijah**. 'Your true God, or Baal.'

WHOOSH

'Here's what we're going to do,' explained **Elijah**. He told the prophets of Baal to build **an altar** to their god, to **cut up** one of the bulls and **put** the meat on their **altar,** but not to light the fire. **He** would do the same and then **they** would pray. Whichever god answered their prayers with fire was the true God. All the **people** agreed.

So the **prophets** of Baal **collected** their stones. **They** built their **altar. They** loaded wood on to the **altar, cut up** the bull and **placed** the meat on top of the wood. Then **they** prayed to Baal. Nothing happened. **They** prayed some more. Nothing happened. **They** prayed a lot more. **They** danced around the altar, **jumping** and **shouting** to Baal. **They** kept it up all morning. But still nothing happened.

'Shout louder,' teased **Elijah**. 'Maybe he's thinking. Perhaps he's busy. Or maybe he's gone on holiday,' **he** laughed. 'He could even be asleep. Do you need to shout louder to wake him up?' **Elijah** called.

As the afternoon passed, **they** shouted louder and **danced** faster, but still nothing happened.

WHOOSH

'Enough,' called **Elijah** as the evening came. **He** called the **people** over to where **he** was standing. He **took** twelve stones, built an **altar, loaded** up the wood, **cut up** the bull and **put** the meat on the **altar**. Then **he** dug a large **trench** around the outside of his **altar. Everyone** was very quiet.

'What's he doing?' the **people** wondered. **They** were about to find out. **Elijah** turned to them and **told** them to get **four** buckets of water. When **they** arrived, **he** asked them to **pour** the water all over the **altar**. Then he told them to do the same again—and again. The altar was soaked and the **trench** was full of water.

WHOOSH

Then **Elijah** prayed. 'Please, God, show these people that you are their true God,' **he** prayed, and, as he did, **fire** fell. The water hissed as it **boiled**. The wood crackled as **it burned**, and **the fire** even **burned** up the stones.

'God is the true God!' the **people** called as **they** knelt down and worshipped God.

'Go home now,' **Elijah** told **Ahab**. 'God is going to make it rain.'

As the **crowd** thinned out and **people** started on their journeys home, **Elijah** sat down with his head between his knees. **He** told his young **servant** to **look** towards the sea.

'I can't see anything,' the **servant** said.

'Go and look again,' said **Elijah. He** did this seven times, and on the seventh time the **servant** said he could see a **tiny cloud** out over the sea.

Soon the sky grew black, the **clouds** grew thick and **heavy rain** began to fall. The drought was over.

WHOOSH

Follow up

Discussion

- Why was Obadiah afraid to tell Ahab where to find Elijah?
- Why did Elijah insist on meeting Ahab?
- Why did Elijah ask the people to pour water all over the altar?
- Why did everyone choose to worship God rather than Baal?

Activity

- On a large piece of craft paper, draw twelve stones in the shape of an altar. Draw the wood that Elijah put on top of the stones. Colour a trench full of water around the base of the altar.
- Using red, yellow and orange finger paints, create the flames that God sent down on to Elijah's altar when he prayed.

Prayer

Father, I know that Elijah trusted you and did as you asked, even when people were trying to harm him. Please help me to trust you, too. Amen

23

Naboth's vineyard

1 KINGS 20—21

characters	objects	sounds
king of Syria	Samaria	
kings of 32 other countries	tents	
Syrian army	Syrian army camp	
Ahab	Israeli army camp	
Ahab's army	vineyard	
messenger	palace	
Ahab's leaders	bedroom	
prophet	feast	
young commanders		
Naboth		
servants		
Jezebel		
people		
city leaders		
two men		
Elijah		
one of Ahab's enemies		

The **king** of Syria, together with 32 other **kings**, called his **army** together to attack **Samaria** in Israel, where **King Ahab** lived. After **his** first attack, the **king** of Syria sent a **messenger** to **Ahab**.

'Give me your best silver and gold,' **he** demanded. **Ahab** decided that this was better than fighting, so **he** agreed.

But then the **messenger** came again.

'New terms,' the messenger **said**. 'The king of Syria wants *all* of your silver and gold, and all of your wives and children.'

'No,' said **Ahab**, angrily.

'You've got 24 hours,' the **messenger** said, 'before the king marches in and helps himself.'

WHOOSH

Ahab called a meeting of his **leaders**. **They** talked about the threat and advised **Ahab** to say 'no'. When **Ahab** refused to give in to the demands, the **king** of Syria said he would reduce everything in Samaria to rubble.

But then a **prophet** of God came to visit **Ahab**.

76

'God says you are to attack,' **he** told Ahab, and because **Ahab** knew that the **prophet** was speaking God's words, that's exactly what **he** did. **He** called his **troops** together, **put** the **young commanders** at the front of the army and **ordered** them into battle. The **king** of Syria, instead of being ready to fight, **was** in his **tent** with the other **kings, getting drunk. His army** was defeated and **he** only just escaped with his life.

WHOOSH

During the winter, **Ahab** trained his **army** and got ready for another battle, because God's **prophet** had said that the king of Syria was going to attack again. Sure enough, when spring came, a **new army** appeared. This time it was much **bigger** and, as it set up **camp**, the **Syrian tents** covered the countryside for miles around. Opposite them, the **Israelites** looked like two tiny flocks of goats.

For **seven days they** faced each other, and then, on the seventh day, came the **battle**. Even though **the Israelites** were outnumbered, **they** won again, and the **king of Syria** was left **pleading** with **Ahab** for his life.

Ahab decided to make a treaty with the **Syrian king**, then **he** let him go.

WHOOSH

Life in **Samaria** was normal again and **people** went about their lives in peace. Some time later, **Ahab** decided that **he** wanted a vegetable garden. **He** looked around and discovered that there was a **vineyard** right next to his **palace**. It would do very nicely.

So off **he** went to the vineyard in search of **Naboth**, the owner. When **Ahab** found him, **he** offered either to **buy** the vineyard or to **give** Naboth another piece of land somewhere else.

'No,' said **Naboth** to the **king**. 'God gave that land to my family a long time ago.'

When **Ahab** heard this, **he** was so angry that **he** marched home, **stormed** into his **bedroom, lay down** on the bed and **sulked** like a little child. **He** even refused to eat when his **servants** brought him food.

WHOOSH

His wife **Jezebel** wondered what was wrong.

'What are you sulking about?' **she** asked. 'And why won't you eat?'

When **Ahab** told her about the **vineyard, she** could hardly believe her ears.

'You're a king,' **she** said. 'Start behaving like one.'

Then **Jezebel** sat down and **wrote** a letter. She told the city leaders to organise a feast, invite Naboth and give him an important place where everyone could see him. Then two liars were to accuse Naboth of cursing God and the king, after which they were to kill him.

So the next day, all the **people** were invited to a **feast** organised by the **city leaders. Naboth** was shown to a seat where **everyone** could see him. And sure enough, during the **feast, two men** stood up and publicly accused **Naboth** of cursing God and the king. Straight away, **Naboth** was taken away from the feast and killed.

Then the **leaders** sent a message to **Jezebel**, who was waiting at the royal palace. 'Naboth is dead,' the message said.

She went straight to **Ahab**.

'Get up,' **she** said. 'Naboth is dead, so you can have the vineyard.' So **Ahab** got out of bed and **went** to take over Naboth's land.

WHOOSH

But **God** wasn't going to let Ahab get away with murder so that he could get something that wasn't his. He told **Elijah** to pay **Ahab** a visit.

'So, you old enemy,' said **Ahab** when **Elijah** arrived in the **vineyard**. 'You've found me.'

'Yes, I have,' said **Elijah**, 'and I have a message from God. Because you have murdered Naboth, you and Jezebel will both die.'

Ahab was the worst king Israel had ever had. **He** worshipped other gods and **he** even killed his own **people** when they refused to worship anyone other than God. Three years later, **Ahab** died during yet another battle with the **king of Syria**. **Jezebel** had **encouraged** the king to turn God's people against him and to **worship** her false gods. **She** died when **one of Ahab's enemies** threw her out of a window.

WHOOSH

Follow up

Discussion

- Why did Ahab do as God said when his city was under attack but not when he wanted the vineyard?
- Why did the city leaders do as Jezebel told them and kill Naboth?
- What sort of person was Ahab?
- Why did God punish Ahab and Jezebel?

Activity

- Draw a large bunch of grapes and colour them either green or purple.
- On each grape, write one thing we do that pleases God.

Prayer

Father God, please help me to remember how you want me to live, and not to follow along with other people when I know that what they are doing is wrong. Amen

24
Elijah and Elisha, prophets of God

1 KINGS 19:1–21; 2 KINGS 2:1–15; 5:1–27

characters	objects	sounds
Elijah	altar	hurricane
people	fire	shattering rocks
Ahab	tree	crackling fire
Jezebel	cave	whirlwind
messenger	hurricane	
angel	rocks	
God	earthquake	
Elisha	fire	
Elisha's parents	camels	
Naaman	Elisha's home	
king of Syria	River Jordan	
servant girl		
king of Israel		
messenger		
Elisha's servant		
Naaman's servants		

Elijah was a prophet who taught people about God. On one occasion, **he** wanted to prove to the **people** of Israel that the gods they worshipped were false, so **he** challenged them to call fire down on an **altar**. **They** couldn't, but when **he** poured water all over his **altar** and then **prayed** to God, **fire** came down and burnt everything. Then the **people** were sorry, because **they** realised that they had broken their promise to follow God.

When **Ahab**, the king, told his wife **Jezebel** about it, **she** was furious. **She** sent a messenger to **Elijah** saying, 'I'll get even with you for this. By this time tomorrow, you'll be a dead man.'

Elijah was terrified and ran for his life.

WHOOSH

Eventually he was so exhausted that **he** had to stop running. **He** sat down under the shade of a **tree** and fell asleep. Suddenly, an **angel** shook him awake and **gave** him a loaf of bread and a jug of water. **Elijah** ate and drank, and fell asleep again. A second time, the **angel** woke him up with food and water. After **he** had eaten, he got up and walked on, for another 40 days. **He** found a cave, crawled into it and fell asleep.

But then there came a voice. 'Elijah, what are you doing here?' **it** asked.

'The people have turned away from you and they're trying to kill me,' said **Elijah**, feeling very sorry for himself.

'Go outside,' said **God**. **Elijah** did as God said, and straight away there was an almighty **hurricane** that ripped through the **rocks** and **shattered** them into tiny pieces. Then there was an **earthquake** that shook the ground beneath Elijah. And then there was a raging **fire**. And after the fire, there was a gentle **voice**.

'So, Elijah, what *are* you doing here?' asked **God** gently.

'They're trying to kill me,' said **Elijah**.

'I know,' said **God**. 'I want you to go back and find a young man called Elisha. He is going to be your helper.'

WHOOSH

Elijah travelled back the way he had come, and almost straight away he found **Elisha** ploughing a field. **Elijah** went up to Elisha and threw his cloak around his shoulders. After saying goodbye to his **parents**, **Elisha** joined **Elijah** on his journey.

Elijah knew that it was nearly time to leave his life on earth. One day, while **they** were out walking, **Elijah** asked **Elisha** what he most wanted.

'To be a holy man like you,' **Elisha** answered. As **they** carried on walking along and talking, a chariot and horses of fire appeared and took **Elijah** away in a **whirlwind**. All that was left was his cloak. **Elisha** wrapped the cloak around himself and **set off** to carry on Elijah's work.

WHOOSH

Naaman was a very important general who had won some important victories for the **king of Syria**. **He** led many raids on Israel. But **he** had a problem: he had a skin disease called leprosy. **He** kept trying to hide it but **he** knew that, as the disease spread, other people would notice and eventually he would die.

One day, his wife's **servant**, a little Israeli girl he had captured during one of the raids, found out about the disease.

'I know someone who could help,' **she** said. 'He's a prophet in my home country.'

Straight away, the **Syrian king** gave **Naaman** permission to visit this prophet and **he** sent **Naaman** on his way with a letter to the king of Israel, asking for his help. **Naaman** left with his **camels** loaded with gold, silver and fine clothes as gifts to whoever could make him better.

WHOOSH

But when **Naaman** arrived, the **king of Israel** was not pleased to see him.

'Do you think I'm God?' **he** yelled when he read the letter. 'I can't make you better.' **He** was frightened that the letter was somehow a plot to start another war.

Just then, a **messenger** came from **Elisha**, telling the **king** to send **Naaman** to him. So off went **Naaman** to Elisha's **home**. **He** was offended when a **servant** came out to speak to him rather than the prophet himself. **He** was even more annoyed when he was told to wash himself in the dirty **River Jordan**, not just once but seven times. **He** was about to go home in disgust, but his **servants** persuaded him to try it.

'What harm can it do?' **they** reasoned, so **Naaman** reluctantly went to the muddy shore of the river.

'One… two… three,' his **servants** counted, until **he** had washed himself seven times. And on the seventh time, **he** came up out of the muddy water with clear, clean skin. The disease was gone.

'The God of Israel really is the true God,' said **Naaman** in amazement. As **he** travelled home, **rejoicing** that his disease had completely gone, **he** promised to follow God for the rest of his life.

WHOOSH

Follow up

Discussion

- Why did Elijah run away?
- Why did Elisha follow Elijah?
- Why didn't Naaman want to wash himself in the River Jordan?
- What did Naaman learn about God?

Activity

- Cut out two identical outlines of a person. Colour one image to show Naaman as a successful army commander. Colour the other to show Naaman covered in a skin disease.
- Stick the images on either side of a lolly stick to create a 'before' and 'after' reminder of how God healed Naaman.

Prayer

Thank you, Father God, that just as you spoke to Elijah and Naaman in a gentle voice, you speak to us very quietly, too. Help me to hear your voice. Amen

5

Jonah and the people of Nineveh

2 KINGS 14:25; JONAH 1—3

characters	objects	sounds
Jonah	Nineveh	howling wind
people	Joppa	creaking masts
king	ships	noise of the storm
God	ship going to Tarshish	
people on the ship	sails	
sailors	waves	
captain	deck	
people of Nineveh	cargo	
king of Iraq	current	
	seaweed	
	fish	

Jonah was a prophet who lived in a town in Israel called Gath Hepher. **He** spent his time **travelling** around Israel, **reminding** people about how God had saved his people from slavery in Egypt and how **they** had made a promise always to love and worship God. Once **he** even spoke to the **king** to tell him that he was setting a bad example to the people.

One day, **God** told **Jonah** that he wanted him to go to **Nineveh**, a huge city in Iraq, more than 500 miles away.

'I want you to tell the people about me. They need to know how much I love them,' **God** said. **Jonah** thought about this for a while, then **he** decided that it didn't seem such a good idea. **He** didn't like the people who lived in Iraq very much, and **he** didn't want to tell them about God. **He** made a plan: he would run away from God.

WHOOSH

So instead of going to Nineveh, **Jonah** went to **Joppa**, a busy port with lots of **ships** coming and going. He found a **ship** heading for Tarshish, hundreds of miles in the opposite direction from Nineveh. **He** paid his fare and **got** on board. **He** was going to get away.

The **ship** set sail, out into the Mediterranean Sea, the **sails** filling with wind. **Jonah** looked back in the direction of Nineveh and **smiled**. There was no way **he** was going there.

But then suddenly the **wind** picked up and started to **howl**. The **masts** started to **creak** and the **waves** got bigger and bigger. The **ship** was thrown around by a huge storm as **waves** swamped the **deck**. It felt as if the wooden ship was going to break into pieces. **Everyone** was terrified, and the **sailors** were all calling out to their gods to save them as **they** struggled to control the **ship**. **They** threw the **cargo** overboard—the heaviest boxes at first, but then everything as the **ship** was tossed violently to and fro.

WHOOSH

Meanwhile, **Jonah**, pleased that his plan had worked, **had gone** below decks for a nap. **He** was fast asleep when the **captain** found him and **shook** him awake.

'Sleeping?' shouted the **captain** above the noise of the storm. 'How can you sleep? Get up and pray to your God. We're all going to drown.'

As **Jonah** went up on deck, the **sailors** were trying to decide whose fault the storm was, so **they** decided to draw straws. It was no surprise to **Jonah** when **he** drew the short straw.

'Who are you?' the **sailors** demanded. 'Why has this happened?'

As **Jonah** told them his story, **they** realised that **he** was running away from God. **They** were terrified and **pleaded** with **Jonah** to do something.

'There's only one thing you can do,' said **Jonah**. 'Throw me overboard, and the storm will stop.'

WHOOSH

For a while, the **sailors** refused. **They** even tried rowing back to shore. But the **waves** were too big and the **wind** was too strong as the **storm** got worse and worse. Eventually, **they** agreed to do what **Jonah** suggested. **They** picked **him** up and threw **him** overboard, and immediately the **storm** stopped. The **waves** were back to normal. The **wind** was silent. The **sailors** realised, then, that Jonah's God was the true God, and **they** all worshipped him. **They** even asked **God** to forgive them for throwing a man to his death.

WHOOSH

As **Jonah** sank into the deep water, **he** was terrified that **he** was going to drown. **Waves** crashed over **him** as **he** came up for air. The **current** pulled him this way and that. **Seaweed** got tangled in his hair, his mouth filled with water, and then **he** sank down and down, **calling** out to God to save him.

And **God** did. **He** sent a huge **fish** to swallow **Jonah** whole. As **he** sat in the stinking belly of the **fish**, **Jonah** realised that he couldn't run away from God. **He** realised that God loved everyone, not just Jonah's people.

'I'm sorry,' **he** said to God. 'I'll do as you told me to.'

And with that, the **fish** spat **Jonah** up on a beach. This time, when **God** said, 'Now, go to **Nineveh** and tell the people there how much I love them,' **Jonah** went, straight away.

WHOOSH

Jonah walked through the **city**. **He** told **everyone** how much God loved them and the **people** listened. **They** told God they were sorry for the bad things they had done. **They** even took off their fine clothes and put on clothes made from rough sacks, to show how sorry they were.

Then the **king** got to hear about it too. Even **he** wore rough clothes, told God how sorry he was and promised to worship God in future. **Everyone** in the city turned away from their evil lives and chose to obey God.

WHOOSH

Follow up

Discussion

- Why did Jonah decide to run away from God?
- What did the sailors learn about God?
- What did Jonah learn about God?
- Why did he decide to go to Nineveh the second time that God told him to?

Activity

- Draw around a saucer to create the profile of a large fish. Add a tail, fin, eye and mouth. Decorate or colour the fish as you wish.
- Cut the fish in two horizontally. Fix the pieces to the top and bottom part of a clothes peg, so that when the peg is opened and closed, the fish opens and closes its mouth and stomach.

Prayer

Father, Jonah learnt that you love absolutely everybody, no matter who they are or what they've done wrong. That includes me—thank you. Amen

26

Jeremiah is given a special job

JEREMIAH 1:1–9, 14–19; 18:1–12; 19:1–15; 24:1—25:14; 32:1–5; 34:1–3; 43:12–16; 40:4–6

characters	objects	sounds
Jeremiah	Jerusalem	
God	temple gate	
people of Israel	potter's house	
priests	clay pots	
potter	two baskets	
Nebuchadnezzar	royal palace	
skilled workers	well	
leaders	temple	
king	walls of Jerusalem	
poor people		
captain of the guard		

Jeremiah was just **going** about his life when **God** spoke to him one day.

'I knew all about you before you were born,' **God** told him. 'I have a special job for you to do. I want you to be a prophet, and to tell my people about me.'

'But I'm only a boy,' answered **Jeremiah**. 'What can I do?'

'I'll tell you where to go and what to say,' **God** told **him**. 'Don't be afraid. I will be with you.'

Then **God** touched **Jeremiah's lips**. 'There,' **he** said. 'I've given you the words to say.'

Jeremiah knew that God's **people** had started worshipping false gods and **they** had forgotten all about their promise to be faithful to God. As **Jeremiah** stood there, **he** knew that God wanted him to warn his people that they must turn back to God.

WHOOSH

So **Jeremiah** set off. When **God** told him to walk up and down the streets of **Jerusalem**, he did. When God told him to stand at the **gate** to the **temple**, he did. **Crowds** would gather and, whenever **he** spoke, **Jeremiah** would say, 'This is the word of the Lord.' **He** would remind people how God had saved them from slavery in Egypt. **He** would remind them how much God loved them. **He** would remind them that they had promised to worship only God. And then **he** would warn them that, if they didn't listen, God was going to punish them.

People didn't really want to change what they were doing, so **they** listened, **shook** their heads, and **walked** away. The **priests** got annoyed with **Jeremiah** and **started** warning people not to take any notice of **him**.

WHOOSH

Another time, **God** told **Jeremiah** to go to the **house** where the **potter** lived. When **he** arrived, there was the **potter**, **sitting** at his wheel, making **clay pots**. **People** started to gather round to watch the **potter** working. Most **pots** would turn out well, but when a **pot** wasn't right, the **potter** would start again, using the same clay.

Jeremiah turned to the **people**. **He** told them that if they didn't turn back to **God, he** would treat them like the wobbly pots and **he** would shape them into new people.

Everyone shook their heads and **walked** away.

Jeremiah even **bought** a clay pot, went back to the **temple gate** and **smashed** the pot to smithereens in front of everyone, as a warning that God would do this to his people if they didn't turn back to him.

Everyone walked away.

WHOOSH

Then, one day, **Nebuchadnezzar**, king of Babylon, invaded Jerusalem. **He** took the **skilled workers** and the **leaders** back to his own country. Later, **Jeremiah** was standing at the temple when he noticed **two baskets** of figs. **One** was full of beautiful ripe fruit, but the figs in the **other basket** were completely rotten.

'The good figs,' said **God**, 'are like the people who have been taken to Babylon. Their lives will be good. They will worship me, and one day I will bring them back to Jerusalem. They will be my people and I will be their God.'

But when **Jeremiah** went to look at the **basket** of bad figs, and then **looked** around at the people left in Jerusalem, **he** realised that they were rotten, just like the figs. **God** told **Jeremiah** to go and warn the **people** that **Nebuchadnezzar** was coming back, and this time **he** was going to destroy their city completely. This time, **everyone** was so angry with **Jeremiah** that the **king** decided to lock him up inside the **royal palace**, to stop him declaring the word of the Lord.

WHOOSH

Still **Jeremiah** didn't stop warning them about what would happen. So **they** threw him down a **well** to try to keep him quiet, and there **he** stayed until **they** got scared that he might die, and **they** pulled him out.

But sure enough, what God had said did happen. **Nebuchadnezzar**, angry with the **king**, mounted an all-out attack on **Jerusalem** and the surrounding towns. By the time he had finished, the **temple** that Solomon had built for the people to worship God lay in **ruins**. Even the **wall of Jerusalem**, their strongest city, lay in piles of **rubble. Everyone** was rounded up and taken to Babylon. Just a few **poor people** were left to farm the land.

And **Jeremiah**? At first **he** was led off in chains with everyone else, but when the **captain of the guard** realised who he was, the chains were removed and **he** was set free. **Jeremiah** went back to his country to live and work with the **people** who had been left behind.

WHOOSH

Follow up

Discussion

- What did God do when Jeremiah said he was too young to speak for God?
- What did Jeremiah tell everyone?
- Why did people treat Jeremiah so badly?
- How do you think people felt when they saw their temple and city walls in ruins?
- What did God promise to the people who were taken captive?

Activity

- Leaving a few centimetres clear at either side of a piece of A4 paper in landscape, write the words of Jeremiah 29:11 and decorate the page with a border. Fix a stick on each of the two short sides of the piece of paper and roll both sides towards the centre to make a scroll.
- Use the scroll to remind yourself of God's message to us through the story of Jeremiah.

Prayer

Thank you, Father, that there are people who can tell us about you and how much you love us. Please help me to listen carefully and help me to understand what they say. Amen

27

Nebuchadnezzar builds a big fire

DANIEL 1—3

characters	objects	sounds
Nebuchadnezzar officials young people Nebuchadnezzar's staff Daniel Shadrach Meshach Abednego God wise men governors leaders servants angel	Jerusalem temple statue furnace	band

Nebuchadnezzar, king of Babylon, declared **war** on the country of Judah. **He** invaded **Jerusalem**, and he even went into the **temple** and removed all the gold and silver cups before **he** destroyed the building. Then **he** took all the finest **officials** and **young people** back to his own country to work for him.

Nebuchadnezzar told his **staff** to **choose** some of the healthiest and most intelligent **young men** that they could find, and train them to work in his government. Four of the young men from Judah—**Daniel, Shadrach, Meshach** and **Abednego**—were among those chosen. **Nebuchadnezzar** ordered **them** to be educated in the Babylonian language and in how to interpret dreams. So **Daniel** and his **friends** read books and learnt all about their new country and its people, but **they** also continued to worship God and follow his rules for their lives.

WHOOSH

Then **Nebuchadnezzar** started having bad dreams. **He** couldn't sleep at night for worrying about them, so he called for his **wise men** to tell him what the dreams meant. One person after another came in, but the **king** wanted them to tell him what he had dreamt, as well as what it meant. When **none** of them could do it, **he** decided to have all his **wise men** killed, even the ones who weren't actually there.

When **Daniel** heard about this, he rushed home to his **friends**. **They** didn't want to be killed, so

they prayed about it and, during the night, **God** told **Daniel** all about the dream and its meaning. The next day, **Daniel** asked one of the king's **officials** to take him to the **king**, so that he could explain the dream.

'Are you sure you can tell me?' asked the **king**. 'Nobody else could.'

'I can, because God in heaven has told me what to say.' **Daniel** didn't only tell the king what **he** had dreamt, but **Daniel** also explained what it meant.

'Your God is definitely the God of all gods,' said **Nebuchadnezzar. He** promoted **Daniel** to become governor of Babylon, **put him** in charge of all the **wise men**, and **gave him** many, many gifts. And when **Daniel** asked the **king** if his **friends** could be given jobs too, **Nebuchadnezzar** gave **them** jobs as administrators.

WHOOSH

Daniel, **Shadrach**, **Meshach** and **Abednego** were very busy working for the king. Even though the Babylonian **people** worshipped other gods, **they** continued to worship the true God. Then, one day, **Nebuchadnezzar** ordered a huge **gold statue** to be made. It was 90 feet high, and the **king** invited all his **officials**, **governors** and **leaders** to a dedication service for his statue. He organised a **band** with trumpets, tubas, trombones, drums and cymbals, and **he** ordered everyone to bow down to his **statue** when the music started.

Shadrach, **Meshach** and **Abednego** were invited to the ceremony, but **they** knew that **they** couldn't bow down to the statue. They could only bow down to God. So when the **music** started, **they** stayed standing. It wasn't long before a group of **people** rushed off to the **king** to tell him what had happened.

WHOOSH

Nebuchadnezzar was furious that someone had disobeyed him, so **Shadrach**, **Meshach** and **Abednego** were ordered to see him.

'Why didn't you bow down to my gold statue?' **he** demanded. When **they** explained why **they** could only bow down to their God, **Nebuchadnezzar** got angry all over again. **He** ordered them to be tied up by their hands and feet and thrown into a burning **furnace. He** gave them one last chance to change their minds, but when **they** refused again, **he** ordered his **servants** to make the roaring **furnace** seven times hotter than normal. When **they** opened it, the flames were so hot that the **servants** died instantly, so there was no hope for **Shadrach**, **Meshach** and **Abednego** as they were thrown in.

WHOOSH

But suddenly, **Nebuchadnezzar** jumped to his feet.

'How many men did we throw into the fire?' he questioned, sounding worried.

'Three, your majesty,' **someone** answered. 'Bound hand and foot.'

'So why are there four in there now?' the **king** demanded.

And sure enough, when **they** looked, there *were* **four men** in the fire, and **they** were walking around. Their hands and feet weren't tied any more.

Nebuchadnezzar rushed over to the furnace.

'Shadrach, Meshach and Abednego, servants of God,' **he** bellowed, 'come out of there!'

And out the **three men** walked, completely unharmed. All the important **leaders, officials** and **government officers** crowded round them and were amazed to find that not only were **they** not harmed, but their clothes weren't scorched and they didn't even smell of smoke.

'Blessed be the God of Shadrach, Meschach and Abednego,' **Nebuchadnezzar** declared, 'because he sent an **angel** to save them from death.'

And straight away, **he** issued a decree saying that if anyone ever said anything against God, they would be killed, and **he** promoted **Shadrach**, **Meshach** and **Abednego** to even more important jobs.

WHOOSH

Follow up

Discussion

- Why did Daniel and his friends worship God, even though they lived with people who worshipped other gods?
- Why do you think Nebuchadnezzar built the golden statue?
- Why did the three friends refuse to kneel down to it?
- What did Nebuchadnezzar learn about God from what happened to the three friends?
- What words would you use to describe the three friends?

Activity

- Cover a piece of A4 paper in tissue-paper flames, allowing them to overlap the edges of the paper.
- Cut out four people in silhouette and stick them on top of the flames.
- Create a headline for the picture—for example, 'Three friends saved by an angel'.

Prayer

Father, help me to make my own choice about belief, not just to follow what other people say. Amen

28

Daniel in the lions' den

DANIEL 5—6

characters	objects	sounds
Belshazzar	feast	hysterical noise
king's staff	fingers	
servants	palace wall	
wise men	banquet hall	
queen	Daniel's house	
Daniel	windows	
Darius	pit of lions	
governors	palace	
angel	dawn	
people in every country		

After **Nebuchadnezzar** died, **Belshazzar** became king. One night, **he** decided to hold a huge **feast** for all his **staff**. There was plenty to eat and drink, and **Belshazzar** had even ordered his servants to bring the gold and silver cups that his father had taken from the temple when he invaded Jerusalem. As **they** drank, **they** praised the gods of gold and silver.

Suddenly, the **fingers** of a human hand appeared and started **writing** on the plaster of the **palace wall**. **Everyone** fell silent and the **king** himself went white as **his** legs gave way beneath him.

Belshazzar screamed for his **wise men** to tell him what the writing meant. In **they** came, but **not one** of them could understand the writing. The **king** shook in terror.

WHOOSH

Hearing the hysterical **noise**, the **queen** came to the **banquet hall**.

'Don't be so alarmed,' **she** soothed. 'Call Daniel, the man your father put in charge of all the wise men. He is wise and intelligent. He will know what it means.'

So **Daniel** was sent for. When **he** arrived, the **king** pleaded with him to explain the writing on the **wall**. **He** promised Daniel a purple robe and a gold chain if he could explain it.

'I'll even make you the third most important person in my kingdom,' **he** promised.

'You can keep your gifts,' **Daniel** answered, 'but I'll tell you what the writing means.'

Daniel pointed to the gold and silver cups.

'They belong to our temple,' **he** said, 'yet you've been using them for a party. You have set yourself up against God.'

Then **he** pointed to the wall. 'It says, *mene mene tekel parsin*,' **Daniel** said. 'It's telling you that God is bringing your reign to an end. Your kingdom will be divided up between other kings.'

Just as Daniel had said, **Belshazzar** died that night. God had brought his time as king to an end.

WHOOSH

Darius became king next. **He** respected **Daniel** greatly. He appointed 120 **governors** for the kingdom, with **three** men in charge of them. **Daniel** was one of the three men, but he was so good at his job that soon **Darius** put **Daniel** in charge of the kingdom.

Straight away, the other **governors** got together to plot against Daniel, discussing how they could find something to use against him. **They** watched **him** carefully, but **they** couldn't find anything to tell tales about. **Daniel** was trustworthy, he worked hard and he set a good example to everyone else.

They were about to give up, when **they** suddenly had an idea. Maybe they could get Daniel out of the way by using his belief in God. So **they** hatched their plot and got ready.

WHOOSH

The **officials** knew that there was no point in criticising Daniel to the king, so **they** tried something different.

'We've agreed,' **they** said to the **king**, 'that for the next 30 days, everyone should pray to you. Anyone who refuses should be thrown into the lions' pit.'

And because **Darius** liked the idea, **he** signed a decree, which meant that it couldn't be changed.

The **governors** were delighted. Off they went to **Daniel's house** to watch. They didn't have long to wait. **Daniel** prayed to God three times each day, and he always opened the upstairs **windows** facing Jerusalem when he prayed. Just as he always did, **Daniel** knelt down and gave thanks to God.

Pleased that their plan had worked, the **officials** rushed straight back to the **king**. 'That decree you signed,' **they** reminded him. 'The one about praying to you.'

'Yes,' said the **king**, nodding. 'I remember. It cannot be changed.'

When **they** told him that **they** had seen Daniel quite openly praying to God, **Darius** realised that he had been tricked, but **he** had to follow the decree that he had signed. Daniel would have to be thrown into the lions' pit.

WHOOSH

So the **king** gave the order. **Daniel** was thrown into a **pit full of lions**, which was covered with a large stone and sealed by the **king**.

Sadly, **Darius** went home to his **palace**. **He** couldn't eat. **He** couldn't sleep. **He** tossed and **he** turned, and as soon as **dawn** started to light the sky, **he** got up and rushed to the **pit**.

'Daniel,' **he** called out, hardly daring to hope. 'Daniel, servant of the living God, has your God rescued you from the lions?'

'Yes,' **he** heard **Daniel** reply. 'God sent an **angel** that closed the mouths of the lions.'

The **king** was overjoyed and **he** ordered his **servants** to lift **Daniel** from the pit straight away. Then **he** issued another order—for the **officials** who had plotted against Daniel to be thrown in instead.

Finally, **he** wrote to all the **people in every country** to tell them that, in his kingdom, Daniel's God would be worshipped as the true God.

WHOOSH

Follow up

Discussion

- What sort of person was Belshazzar? Why did God say that his reign as king should end?
- In what ways was Darius a different king from Belshazzar?
- Why did he have to throw Daniel into the lions' pit?
- How did God care for Daniel?
- What did Darius learn about God, and what did he do about it?

Activity

- With a piece of white wax candle, draw a lion or write the words '*mene mene tekel parsin*'.
- Colourwash the paper with water-based paint to see the image or words appear on the page.

Prayer

Father, thank you for what I've learnt about you from Daniel's life. Help me as I think about what it means and how I can worship you in my own life. Amen

29

Esther saves the day

ESTHER 1—2; 3—6

characters	objects	sounds
Xerxes	party	
everyone	one week	
servants	royal palace garden	
adviser	couches	
officials	palace	
Mordecai	palace gate	
Esther	room	
Hegai	Haman's home	
seven servants	banquet	
two men	prison	
Haman		

Xerxes, King of Persia, decided to throw a **party**. This wasn't just any party. It was going to be the biggest party ever.

For a whole **week**, absolutely **everyone**, from the most to the least important person in the city of Susa, was invited to the party in the **garden** of the **royal palace**. The **garden** was decorated with silver and gold **couches**. Drinks were served in solid gold cups, each one with its own design. At the order of the **king**, **everyone** could eat and drink as much as they liked—for a whole week! **Servants** were ready to fill up the gold cups with wine whenever anyone asked them.

After his party was over, the **king** decided that he needed a wife.

WHOOSH

The king's **adviser** suggested that the **king** should send a message to every corner of his kingdom, inviting the most beautiful girls to stay at the palace so that he could choose one as his wife. The **king** was pleased with this idea, so he sent his **officials** out with the message.

In the **palace** lived a Jewish man called **Mordecai. He** had adopted **Esther** when her parents died, and had brought her up as his daughter. **Esther** was beautiful, and **she** was one of the girls chosen to meet the king.

Hegai was appointed to look after the girls, because, before any of them could meet the king, **they** had to have a year of beauty treatments and special food. **Hegai** liked Esther very much, so, as well as **organising** her beauty **treatments, Hegai** gave **Esther seven servants** of her own. After a year, it was her turn to **get ready** to meet the king.

WHOOSH

The **king** quickly fell in love with **Esther** and **he** chose **her** as his **wife**. **He** put a royal crown on **her** head, **he** threw another enormous **party**, **he** declared a day's holiday, and **he** gave presents to everyone as if money didn't matter.

One day, **Mordecai** was sitting at the **palace gate** when he overheard **two men** plotting to kill the king. Straight away, he told **Esther**. **She** told the **king**, and the **men** were arrested. The **king** wrote down all the details in his diary.

Some time later, the **king** promoted one of his officials, **Haman**, to be the most important official in the kingdom. **Haman** was very proud, and **he** insisted that **everyone** should kneel when **he** walked past them. But **Mordecai** refused and that made **Haman** very angry. **He** decided that something needed to be done not just about Mordecai, but about all the Jews. So **he** persuaded the **king** to issue a decree that all the Jews should be killed on a single day.

WHOOSH

When **Mordecai** heard this, he went to visit **Esther**. Although she was scared, because she could be killed for going to see the king without being invited, **she** went to stand at the door of the **room** where **he** was sitting on his throne. Because **he** loved **Esther** very much, **Xerxes** called her in and asked her what she wanted.

'I am having a banquet tomorrow,' **she** said, 'and I would like you to come. Please bring Haman with you.'

That night, the **king** couldn't sleep, so **he** called for his diary to be **read** to him. When **he** heard about Mordecai saving his life, **he** realised that he had never rewarded him. So **he** sent for **Haman** and asked him what the king should do for someone he wanted to honour. Thinking that the king meant him, **Haman** suggested a royal robe and one of the king's horses as gifts. When **he** discovered that these were actually for Mordecai, not for him, **he** was furious. To make it even worse, the **king** ordered **Haman** to walk through the city, leading **Mordecai** on the horse, declaring, 'This is the man the king wants to honour.' **Haman's** rage boiled over when he went **home** afterwards. But **he** cheered up when **he** remembered that he was to be a guest of honour at the queen's banquet that evening.

WHOOSH

The food at the **banquet** was delicious. **Haman** was feeling very pleased with himself and, even though he was still furious with Mordecai, **he** knew that all the Jews would soon be dead.

But just as things were looking good, **he** heard the **king** ask **Esther** what she would like as a gift.

'If it pleases you, give me my life, and give my people their lives,' **she** answered. Then **Esther** explained that she was a Jew, and so she would soon be killed. The **king** was angry and **asked** who had dared to think of killing the queen. When **she** pointed to **Haman**, the **king** had **him** arrested and thrown into **prison**.

Xerxes ordered that the Jews could defend themselves against anybody who tried to harm them. **Esther** was given **Haman's house** and land, and **Mordecai** was promoted to his job. So **Mordecai** became the most important official in Persia and Esther had saved her people.

WHOOSH

Follow up

Discussion

- What kind of person was the king?
- Why do you think he loved Esther so much?
- How did Esther save her people?

Activity

Esther's saving of her people is remembered in the Jewish festival of Purim. The story of Esther is read, and children use a gragger, or noise maker, to drown out the name of Haman every time it is mentioned.

To make a gragger, fill an empty drink bottle with anything that rattles, such as rice or pasta. Fix the lid on firmly. Decorate the bottle and shake it hard every time you hear the name of Haman.

Prayer

Father, please help me, just like Esther, to care about people who are threatened because of who they are. Amen

30

Nehemiah rebuilds a wall

2 KINGS 18—19; 24:1–14; NEHEMIAH 1—2; 4; 6:1—7:3

characters	objects	sounds
Hezekiah Sennacherib troops people of Jerusalem Nebuchadnezzar king leaders wealthy people poor people Nehemiah brother Artaxerxes servants work teams enemies	buildings shrines city walls temple Jerusalem rubble	

Hezekiah was one of the best kings that Israel ever had. **He** trusted God and **he** destroyed all the **buildings** and **shrines** that the people had built to worship false gods. Because he trusted God, God stayed close to him, especially when things went wrong.

Israel faced one very determined enemy, **Sennacherib**, king of Assyria. **He** often raided towns and cities in Israel, but one day **he** decided to attack Jerusalem, the capital city.

Soon **he** had the **city walls** surrounded with his **troops**.

'Don't listen to Hezekiah,' **his** men called out to the **people** inside the city. 'God can't save you.' But the **people** said nothing. **They** waited and trusted God.

All night, **Hezekiah** knelt in the **temple** and **prayed** that God would deliver Jerusalem and his **people** from invasion. And that was just how it happened. When the **people** looked over their strong **city walls** the next morning, the whole **Assyrian army** lay dead. Only **Sennacherib** was left alive and he was riding away as fast as he could.

WHOOSH

But after **Hezekiah** died, the **people** returned to their old ways. This time it was **Nebuchadnezzar**, the king of Babylon, who invaded. And when the **king** of Israel rebelled, **Nebuchadnezzar** invaded Jerusalem itself. He took all the gold and silver that he could find. **He** took all the **leaders** and

wealthy people who lived in Israel. All **he** left behind were **poor people**, who were told to farm the land.

By the time **Nebuchadnezzar** had finished, the **temple** and the strong, secure **walls** of the city of Jerusalem lay in **ruins**.

And so, for many years, the **people** of Israel lived in Babylon, ruled over by a foreign **king** who had no time for their God.

WHOOSH

Nehemiah had lived in Babylon for more than 20 years. During all of that time, **he** had trusted and worshipped God, even though **he** lived in a foreign land where **people** worshipped other gods. **He** worked hard and was so well respected that **he** had become the **king**'s cupbearer. **He** was a trusted royal servant and **he** spent every day in the **king**'s presence.

One day, Nehemiah's **brother** came to visit. **He** brought sad news from Jerusalem. The **people** were living in terrible conditions. Jerusalem's **city wall**, which had once been so strong, was still a pile of **rubble. Nobody** had the energy to rebuild it.

When **Nehemiah** heard this, **he** sat down and cried—for days. But **he** didn't just weep; **he** worshipped God too. **He** asked God what **he** could do to help his people. And as **he** prayed, **he** formed a plan.

WHOOSH

One day, when **Nehemiah** was standing next to the **king**, ready to **serve** him with his wine, the king noticed that **Nehemiah** was looking really miserable.

'Why the long face?' asked **Artaxerxes**; it was a crime to be unhappy in front of the king. **Nehemiah** seized his chance. **He** explained about the **city wall** around Jerusalem and about the suffering of his **people**.

'So what can I do?' asked the **king**. **Nehemiah** quickly **prayed** to God, then **acted** boldly. **He** asked for permission to go home and rebuild the wall. **He** asked for building materials. And **he** even asked for a letter from the king, to keep him safe as he travelled.

WHOOSH

And so it was that **Nehemiah** set out for **Jerusalem**, with a letter from the king, permission to rebuild, and letters to all sorts of people telling them to give him the wood he needed to rebuild the city wall. It took a long time to get home, and when **he** did, **Nehemiah** found that the **walls** really were just piles of **rubble**. Before **he** could do anything, **he** would have to survey what was left and make a **plan** to repair the walls.

So, in the middle of the night, **Nehemiah** took some **servants** and **worked** out what needed to be done. **He** scrambled over piles of rubble. **He** measured the gaps where the city gates had been. **He** drew up plans. Then **he** called the **people** together.

'Our great city is in ruins,' **he** told them. 'Let's rebuild, and trust God to help us.'

WHOOSH

Nehemiah organised **work teams** and the rebuilding began. But Nehemiah had powerful **enemies**, who didn't like what they saw. **They** didn't like it at all. **They** sent nasty letters to **Nehemiah**. **They** made threats. **They** tried to get him to meet them outside Jerusalem so that they could kill him. **They** plotted and they planned. And **Nehemiah** just kept right on building, working alongside his **people**.

Furious, his **enemies** tried to attack. So **Nehemiah** gave the **people** weapons. **They** built with tools in one hand and a sword in the other hand, ready for attack. Eventually, **they** even slept in their work clothes. When **they** got discouraged, **Nehemiah** reminded them that God was with them. And in just over seven weeks, the **walls** were finished. Jerusalem was strong again.

WHOOSH

Follow up

Discussion

- Why did God bless Hezekiah and save Jerusalem from invasion?
- Why were the temple and the city wall eventually destroyed?
- In what ways did Nehemiah show that he trusted God?
- Why did Nehemiah pray so often?

Activity

- Discuss things that the children want to pray about, for themselves and others.
- Give each child some brown paper 'bricks' and invite them to write a prayer or draw a prayer picture on each brick. Together, stick the bricks on to a large sheet of paper to make a prayer wall.

Prayer

Father, just as Nehemiah trusted you to help him with something that seemed impossible, please help me to trust you when things seem too hard for me to achieve. Amen

New Testament: the life of Jesus

> Go and tell the disciples to meet me in Galilee.

31

Elizabeth and Zechariah

LUKE 1

characters	objects	sounds
Zechariah Elizabeth Herod Aaron people at the temple priests Gabriel Mary Joseph friends and neighbours people Isaiah Malachi	hill country temple Zechariah's home Nazareth desert	

Zechariah and his wife **Elizabeth** were good people. They lived in the **hill country** of Judea, where **Herod** was the king. **They** worshipped God and kept the rules that he had given his people to live by, hundreds of years earlier. **Elizabeth** could trace her family all the way back to Moses' brother **Aaron**, and **Zechariah** was a priest in the **temple**.

Every day, **Zechariah** would carry out his **temple** duties. One day, something startling happened. **Everyone** was outside, **waiting** to come in and start their prayers. **Zechariah** had been chosen by the other **priests** to burn the incense and he was just getting everything ready inside the **temple** when **Gabriel**, an angel, suddenly appeared. **Zechariah** was terrified.

'Don't be afraid,' the **angel** said. 'I've come to tell you that you and Elizabeth are going to have a baby. You are to call him John.' The **angel** went on to explain that this was a special baby, who would be like their ancient prophet Elijah. He would prepare people for God.

Zechariah and Elizabeth didn't have any children, and **Zechariah** didn't think that what the angel was telling him was likely to happen now, because **they** were both old people. Eventually, **he** managed to say, 'But we're too old to have children.'

Because **Zechariah** didn't believe the angel, **he** was told that he wouldn't be able to speak again until after the baby was born. Outside, the **people** were starting to get restless and they wondered what was keeping Zechariah such a long time. But when **he** came out unable to speak, and had to communicate in **sign language**, **they** realised that he had seen a vision. As soon as prayers in the **temple** were finished and **Zechariah** had performed all his duties, he rushed **home**.

WHOOSH

And it came true, just as Gabriel, God's angel, had told him. One day, **Elizabeth** told **Zechariah** that they were going to have a baby. **They** were both overjoyed.

Elizabeth had a cousin, **Mary**, who lived in **Nazareth**, a town in a different part of the country. **She** was engaged to a man called **Joseph**, and **she** was looking forward to getting married. One day, while **Mary** was going about her work, **Gabriel** appeared to her, too.

'Greetings,' the **angel** said. 'The Lord is with you.'

Mary was scared. What did this mean? Why was an angel appearing to her? **Gabriel** went on to explain that she was going to have a baby. He was to be called Jesus, and he would be the Son of God. The angel even told Mary about Elizabeth's baby.

'Nothing is impossible with God,' **Gabriel** reminded her.

'I am the Lord's servant,' said **Mary**, as the angel disappeared.

WHOOSH

Quickly, **Mary** got ready to go and stay with her cousin, **Elizabeth**. It was a long journey—over 80 miles—but **Mary** was in a hurry to see her cousin, and when she arrived at their **home**, **Elizabeth** was delighted to see her.

'Blessed are you among women,' **she** said as she hugged **Mary**, and **together** they praised God for everything that was going to happen. **Mary** stayed with **Elizabeth** and **Zechariah** for three months, **sharing** with them as **they** prepared for their baby to be born. But all too soon, it was time for **Mary** to go home.

WHOOSH

Soon afterwards, **Elizabeth** and **Zechariah's baby** was born, and their **friends** and **neighbours** all wanted to celebrate the baby's birth with them. When **people** came to visit, they assumed that he was going to be called Zechariah, after his father.

'No, no,' said **Elizabeth**. 'His name is John.'

Everyone was puzzled. There was nobody in the family called John, so why would they choose the name? **They** turned to **Zechariah** and **asked** him what **he** wanted to call the baby, but **he** still couldn't speak. So **he** asked for a slate, and on it, to **everyone's** amazement, **he** wrote, 'His name is John.'

Immediately, **Zechariah** could speak again. All their **neighbours** were astonished by what had happened, and news about it spread to **people** for miles around.

'What sort of child is he going to be?' **they** asked each other. 'God is with him.'

But **Zechariah** knew why **his son** had been born. **He** remembered their ancient prophet, **Isaiah**, who had said that there would be a voice in the desert, calling, 'Prepare the way for the Lord.' **He** remembered, too, their ancient prophet **Malachi**, who had said, 'God is going to send a messenger to clear the way.'

'The Lord is coming to show us the way to God,' **Zechariah** said to his **baby son**, 'and you will go ahead of him and prepare his way.'

Elizabeth and **Zechariah** watched **John** grow up to be healthy, strong and lively. And then, to prepare for his life doing God's work, **John** went to live in the desert. **He** ate locusts and wild honey, dressed himself in clothes made from camel skins and wore a leather belt around his waist. There **he** stayed until it was time for him to start the work that God wanted him to do.

WHOOSH

Follow up

Discussion

- Why didn't Zechariah believe what the angel told him?
- What happened as a result?
- Why do you think Mary was so keen to go and visit her cousin Elizabeth?
- After John was born, how did Zechariah know what work John was going to do for God?

Activity

The prophet Isaiah said that someone would prepare the way for the Lord before he came to earth. Design a poster preparing people for Jesus coming to earth to share the good news of God's kingdom.

Prayer

Thank you, Father, that you send messengers so that we can learn about you and your kingdom. Help me to listen and understand. Amen

32

Jesus is born

MATTHEW 1:18—2:23; LUKE 2:1–20

characters	objects	sounds
Mary	Bethlehem	
Joseph	Nazareth	
Gabriel	manger	
Romans	fields	
Caesar Augustus	sheep	
everyone in Israel	fire	
innkeepers	star	
baby	Jerusalem	
shepherds	Egypt	
angel		
choir of angels		
everyone the shepherds met		
wise men		
Herod		
priests		
scholars		
Herod's guards		

Mary and **Joseph** were going to be married. One day, while **Mary** was going about her work, an **angel** from God visited her. The angel **Gabriel** told **Mary** that she was going to have a baby—but this was a very special baby. He was to be called Jesus, and he would be the Son of God. An **angel** told **Joseph** about the baby, too, in a **dream** one night.

'Call him Jesus,' the **angel** said, 'because he will save my people from their sins.'

Israel, the country where Mary and Joseph lived, was occupied by the **Romans**. **Caesar Augustus**, the Roman emperor, decided that he wanted to hold a census, to count exactly how many people lived in the country. **Everyone** had to go to their family home.

WHOOSH

Joseph had to travel to **Bethlehem** because he could trace his family all the way back to King David, who had been born in Bethlehem. **Mary** and **Joseph** packed their bags ready for the long, 70-mile walk from their home in Nazareth.

It was nearly time for **Mary's** baby to be born, but **she** still had to make the tiring journey to be registered with Joseph. Then, when **they** arrived, they couldn't find anywhere to stay. **They** tried one inn. **They** tried another inn. 'Sorry, we're full,' the **innkeepers** all said. So when the **baby** was born, **Mary** had to wrap him in a blanket and put him in a **manger** to sleep, because they had nowhere to stay.

WHOOSH

The **fields** around Bethlehem were full of **sheep**, and their **shepherds** were getting ready for the night. The **shepherds** who were on the first watch **checked** that they had their staffs and slingshots, in case any wild animals tried to attack their sheep. The rest of the **shepherds** made sure that there were enough sticks and roots to keep the **fire** burning, before **they** lay down around the **fire** to sleep. Suddenly, the **fields** blazed with light and an **angel** was standing right there with them. **They** were all terrified. But the **angel** just said, 'Don't be afraid. I'm here with good news,' and, **pointing** to the town, the **angel** told them that their Saviour had just been born and that **he** was lying in a manger, wrapped in a blanket.

Before the **shepherds** could say anything, the sky was filled with a huge **choir of angels**, all singing praises to God. There was no thought of sleep now!

'Let's get to Bethlehem as fast as we can,' **they** agreed. 'Let's see for ourselves.'

And with that, **they** ran into **Bethlehem**. **They** found that it was just as the angel had said, and **they** were so excited that they told **everyone** they met what the angel had said about the baby in the manger.

Everyone was very impressed. While **Mary** was left to think about everything that the angels had told the shepherds, **they** jumped and danced and praised God all the way back to their sheep.

WHOOSH

But the shepherds weren't the only people to visit the baby. **Wise men** living in the east had seen a special **star** in the sky before Jesus was born and **they** had set out on their camels to find him and worship him.

Their journey took them through **Jerusalem**, where **they** stopped to rest.

'Where is the baby?' **they** asked. 'The one who is king of the Jews?'

News of their questions reached **Herod** the king, and **he** was very worried. **He** called together all the **priests** and **scholars** and asked them where the Messiah was going to be born. **They** searched the ancient Jewish writings. 'Bethlehem,' one of them said. Then **Herod** got really scared. A king? For the Jews? Somewhere in Bethlehem? That would never do. So **he** asked the wise men to visit him secretly.

'The baby is in Bethlehem,' **he** told them. 'When you find him, let me know, so that I can come and worship him, too.'

As the **wise men** left **Jerusalem**, the **star** appeared again and **led** them right to the place where the **baby** was. **They** gave Jesus gifts of gold, incense and myrrh and **they** bowed down and worshipped him. Then, having been **warned in a dream** not to go back to Herod, **they** left Bethlehem and went home by a different way.

WHOOSH

After the **wise men** had left, an **angel** spoke to **Joseph** again, while he was asleep.

'Get up,' the **angel** said. 'Take **Mary** and **Jesus** and run for your lives into **Egypt**.' So there **they** were, in the middle of the night, **running away** from Herod.

And it was as well that they did, because when **Herod** heard that the wise men had gone home by a different way, **he** was so angry that **he** ordered his **guards** to **kill** every baby boy in Bethlehem.

Joseph, **Mary** and **Jesus** stayed safely in Egypt until **Herod** died. Then the **angel** visited **Joseph** again and told him that it was safe to go back to Israel.

And so it was that **they** finally arrived home. **They** had gone to **Bethlehem** for a census and ended up living in **Egypt**!

Mary and **Joseph** cared for their special **son** as he grew up.

WHOOSH

Follow up

Discussion

- What sort of people were Mary and Joseph? How do we know?
- Why was Herod so frightened?
- How did the shepherds and wise men show that they trusted God?

Activity

Make a baby card to welcome Jesus. Remember, when you design the card, that Jesus was born with a purpose and had special work to do for God.

Prayer

Jesus, thank you for coming to earth to tell us the good news about the kingdom of God. Amen

33

Jesus meets John the Baptist

MATTHEW 3:1–17; MARK 1:1–11; LUKE 3:1–22; JOHN 1:15–34

characters	objects	sounds
Isaiah people of Israel messenger Elizabeth Zechariah John Romans Emperor Tiberius Pontius Pilate King Herod tax collectors soldiers Jewish leaders priests Jesus, the Son of God	temple desert River Jordan Jerusalem sky dove	voice of God

Long ago, in Israel, there lived a prophet of God called **Isaiah. He** told people about God and the rules that God had given them to live by. Every time the **people of Israel** forgot about God, **Isaiah** would remind them to turn back to God.

One day, **Isaiah** told the people, 'A **messenger** is shouting in the desert. He is saying, "Prepare a straight path and get ready for the Lord!"' **Everyone** looked at each other and **wondered** what it meant, but **nobody** seemed to know.

Many of the things that **Isaiah** said were **written down** on scrolls and **people** carried on reading them in the **temple** long after Isaiah had died. It was to be 700 years before anyone really understood what he had meant about the voice calling out in the desert.

WHOOSH

Elizabeth and **Zechariah** had only one child—**John**, who had been born when they were very old. **Zechariah** knew that his son was a very special gift from God and that God had very special work for him to do. As **he** read the scroll of Isaiah in the **temple**, he knew that **John** was going to be the person that Isaiah had written about, all those years ago. **His son** was going to live in the desert and was going to prepare the way for the Lord.

And so **they** watched as their son grew into a strong and lively young man. Then, one day, just as the ancient prophecy had said, **John** went to live in the **desert**. His clothes were made out of camel skins and were pulled together around him with a leather belt. He lived on locusts and wild honey. It was time for **him** to start his work for God.

WHOOSH

'Turn back to God,' **John** told **people**. 'The kingdom of God is coming.' **Crowds** of people flocked from Jerusalem and all over Judea to hear **John** speak. **They** liked the sound of God's kingdom. **They** were fed up with being occupied by the **Romans** and governed by **Emperor Tiberius** in Rome, **Pontius Pilate** in Judea and **King Herod** in Galilee. **They** wanted to be freed.

But **John** wasn't talking about the kingdom of Israel. **He** was talking about the kingdom of heaven.

'Turn back to God,' **John** said, 'and your sins will be forgiven.'

'What should we do?' **people** asked. 'How should we live?'

'If you've got two coats, give one away to someone who doesn't have one,' answered **John**. 'If you've got some food, share it.'

When **people** told God they were sorry, **John** baptised them, right there in the **River Jordan**.

WHOOSH

One day, some **tax collectors** came to talk to John and asked to be baptised. 'What should we do?' **they** asked him.

'Don't make people pay any more money than they really owe,' answered **John**. Then some **soldiers** who were there asked him what they should do.

'Don't force people to pay you money to leave them alone,' **John** told them. **He** shared the good news with **everyone** who came to listen. **People** got very excited.

'Is this our Messiah?' **they** all started asking each other.

The **Jewish leaders** in **Jerusalem** wanted to know who he really was, so they sent **priests** to ask John.

'I'm not the Messiah,' **he** told them.

'Are you Elijah?' **they** asked. 'Or are you the Prophet?'

'No, neither of those,' **John** replied.

'Well, who are you, then? Tell us. We've got to give an answer to the authorities,' **they** pleaded.

John answered them using the words of the ancient prophet, Isaiah.

'I am the one shouting in the desert, "Prepare the way for the Lord."'

WHOOSH

The next day started like a normal day. **John** was talking to the **crowds** as usual and was **baptising** people, when **he** suddenly saw **Jesus** approaching him. **John** stopped what he was doing.

'This is the person I'm preparing the way for,' **he** told everyone. 'He is the Son of God. I'm not even worthy to kneel down and undo his sandals. He will take away your sin.'

'I have come to be baptised,' said **Jesus** as he greeted **John**. At first, **John** refused to baptise Jesus.

'It should be the other way round,' **he** said. 'You should baptise me.'

But **Jesus** insisted. 'We must do all that God wants us to do,' **he** said gently to **John**.

So together **they** went down in the water of the **River Jordan**, and **John** baptised **Jesus**, just as he had baptised many other people.

But this time it was very different. As soon as **Jesus** came up out of the water, the **sky** was torn apart and the Holy Spirit came down, looking like a **dove**.

'This is my own special Son,' a **voice** said from heaven. 'I am very pleased with him.' Then **people** understood what **John** had meant when he said he was preparing the way for someone much greater than himself. **He** was preparing the way for the **Son of God**.

WHOOSH

Follow up

Discussion

- How did John know that God wanted him to do a special job? How did he get ready for it?
- Why were the Jewish leaders so interested in who John was?
- Why didn't John want to baptise Jesus?
- What did the people understand after they had seen Jesus being baptised?

Activity

Design a road sign showing the message that John was sharing—that Jesus is the way to God. Remember that road signs giving information are usually white on a blue background.

Prayer

Thank you, Father, that your Son Jesus came to earth to show us the way to you. Help me to learn more about Jesus. Amen

34

Jesus in the wilderness

MATTHEW 4:1–11; MARK 1:12–14; LUKE 4:1–14

characters	objects	sounds
John the Baptist crowds Jesus voice angels the devil powerful kings and rulers people Herod Philip Herodias	desert River Jordan dove scorching hot/freezing cold wild animals scorpions stones mountain Jerusalem temple prison Jesus' home	

John the Baptist lived in the **desert**, and he drew large **crowds** of people whenever he spoke. **They** flocked from Jerusalem and all around Judea. **John** told them that **they** should tell God they were sorry for the things they had done that were wrong, and that **they** should be looking for their Messiah, the person who could save them from their sins.

'I'm not even worthy to kneel down and undo his sandals,' **John** said about this man. Then, one day, **Jesus** came to **John** as he was baptising people in the **River Jordan**.

'Baptise me, too,' said **Jesus**, and when **he** came up out of the water, the Holy Spirit came out of the sky like a **dove** and a **voice** from heaven said, 'This is my own special Son. I am very pleased with him.'

After that, **Jesus** went into the **desert** himself. He was about 30 years old, and it was almost time for him to start the work that God had sent him to earth to do. He needed to get ready.

WHOOSH

Jesus stayed in the **desert** for 40 days. The daytimes were **scorching hot**. The night-times were **freezing cold**. All the time, there was danger from **wild animals** and **scorpions**, but **angels** took care of him and he came to no harm. During the whole 40 days, **Jesus** didn't eat, so, at the end of the time, **he** was very, very hungry.

'So you're the Son of God, are you?' the **devil** taunted him. 'Well, since you're so hungry, why don't you just turn these **stones** into loaves of bread?'

Jesus looked at the **stones** around him. **He** was very hungry. **He** knew that he could turn the

stones into food. But **he** also knew that God didn't want him to do that, so **he** thought about the scriptures and what God had to say. **He** knew that it wasn't just about food.

'Nobody can live on just food,' **Jesus** said. 'People need to hear every word that God speaks as well.'

WHOOSH

Next, the **devil** took **Jesus** to a very high **mountain** in the **desert**. **He** showed **Jesus** every country on earth, and Jesus could see all the power that their **kings** and **rulers** held.

'I'll give all this power to you if you want,' the **devil** said to **Jesus**. 'It's mine to give away. All you have to do is worship me.'

Jesus looked at all the countries on earth and all the power that their **kings** and **rulers** held. **He** knew that his Father God was greater even than all these powers combined. So **he** thought about the scriptures again, and this time **he** said, 'Worship and serve only the Lord your God.'

WHOOSH

Finally, the **devil** took **Jesus** into **Jerusalem**. **He** had **Jesus** stand on the very highest part of the **temple**. Then the **devil** said, 'So you think you're the Son of God? Jump off, then.' The **devil** even quoted scripture at **him** this time, **reminding him** that God would send **angels** to catch him so that he wouldn't be killed. **He** wouldn't even hurt his feet as **he** landed on the stones below. **Jesus** knew that this was true. **He** knew that God could send **angels** to save him from being hurt. But **he** also knew it was wrong to do as the devil wanted, just to prove that he really was the Son of God.

'Go away, Satan,' **Jesus** said. For the final time, **Jesus** thought about scripture, and **he** reminded the **devil** that scripture says, 'Don't try to test God.' And after that, the **devil** gave up for a while and left **Jesus** alone.

Then the **angels** came again and helped him.

WHOOSH

Meanwhile, **John** the Baptist had carried on sharing the good news about Jesus, who had come to save people from their sins. **He** carried on telling **people** when their lives were upsetting God. And then one day, **John** spoke to **Herod**, the king of Judea. **Herod** had a brother, **Philip**, who was also an important ruler. When **Herod** had visited his **brother**, he had decided that he preferred Philip's wife, **Herodias**, to the **wife** he had already married. And because **he** was used to getting what **he** wanted, **he** had made **Philip** divorce **Herodias** so that **he** could marry her himself. That was against God's rules, and **John** the Baptist told **Herod** so, even though it made **Herod** very angry. Herod had done many bad things in his life, and **he** added to the list of bad things he had done by locking **John** up in **prison**.

Jesus heard that **John** had been thrown into **prison**. **He** knew it was time for him to start the work that God had sent him to earth to do, so **he** left **Jerusalem** and went **home** to Galilee, ready to start telling everyone about the kingdom of God.

WHOOSH

Follow up

Discussion

- How do we know the difference between right and wrong?
- What did Jesus do when he was tempted to do something wrong?
- What can we learn from Jesus' example?

Activity

- Provide each child with an A4 piece of paper, with the words 'Worship the Lord your God' written on it in outline.
- Add a little glue to different coloured paints. Paint all the letters and cover them in sand while the paint is still wet. Shake off the excess sand.

Prayer

Father, thank you for Jesus' example of what to do when we are tempted to do something wrong. Help me to read the Bible and learn about you, so that when I am tempted I can think about what pleases you. Amen

35

Jesus' last week

MATTHEW 21:1–13; 26:1—27:53; MARK 11:1–19; 14:1—15:39;
LUKE 19:28–48; 22:1—23:49; JOHN 13:1–30; 18:1—19:30

characters	objects	sounds
people	temple	earthquake
Jesus	village	
disciples	donkey	
priests and leaders	Passover meal	
woman	Garden of Gethsemane	
Judas Iscariot	gate	
Peter and John	curtain	
angry mob		
high priest		
Roman guard		

Every year, the **people** of Israel went to the **temple** in Jerusalem for their Passover festival. It was a time when they celebrated their freedom from slavery in Egypt. **Jesus** and his **disciples** were walking to Jerusalem for Passover when **Jesus** suddenly stopped just outside the city. **He** told **two** of his disciples to go ahead to the next **village** and look for a **donkey** tied up outside a house.

'Untie the **donkey** and bring it back,' **he** told them. 'If anyone asks what you're doing, just say, "The Lord needs it."' So off **they** went and found the **donkey**. When they got back to where **Jesus** was waiting, **they** covered it with their own clothes. **Jesus** got on and headed into the city. Everywhere **he** went, **people** cut palm branches from trees and waved them, shouting, 'Hosanna! Hosanna!'

'What's all the fuss?' some **people** asked. 'Who is it?'

'Jesus, the prophet from Nazareth,' **others** answered, waving their palm branches even harder.

WHOOSH

As **Jesus** entered Jerusalem, the **crowds** continued to cheer. But when Jesus arrived at the **temple**, **he** was very angry, because **people** were selling things there and making a lot of money. Getting off the donkey, he strode into the temple, turning over the tables and scattering money and goods everywhere.

'My house is a place of worship,' **he** told them all, 'but you have turned it into a place where robbers hide.'

Afterwards, **Jesus** stayed in the **temple**, teaching people about God. **Everyone** crowded in to hear him speak. It was the same every day: **Jesus** taught and **crowds** came to listen.

WHOOSH

The **priests** and **leaders** were getting annoyed with **Jesus**. **They** met together and tried to plot a way to kill him. In the end, **they** decided that it was too dangerous, because Jesus was so popular with everyone who was visiting Jerusalem for Passover. **They** would just have to wait.

But their chance came sooner than they might have hoped. One evening, **Jesus** was having a meal when a **woman** came into the room. **She** knelt down and poured a bottle of expensive perfume all over **Jesus**' feet. The **disciples** were cross with **her** for wasting money, but **Jesus** just looked at them and said, 'She has poured perfume on my body ready for my burial.'

Soon afterwards, **Judas Iscariot**, one of the disciples, sneaked off to the **priests**. 'How much money will you give me if I help you arrest him?' **Judas** asked. **They** agreed to give him 30 silver coins, and **Judas** went back to join the **disciples** as if nothing had happened.

WHOOSH

Peter and **John**, meanwhile, were getting ready for the **Passover meal**, in a large upstairs room of a house in Jerusalem. When it was time to eat, **Jesus** and his **disciples** arrived. **Jesus** broke the bread, gave a piece to each of them, and told them to eat it as a way of remembering him. Then **he** took the wine, but, before he shared it, **he** told them that he was going to die and that one of them would betray him. The **disciples** got upset and started arguing about who would do such a thing. Then **Jesus** dipped a piece of bread in the wine and gave it to **Judas**. **Judas** took the bread and went out.

WHOOSH

After the meal, **Jesus** and his **disciples** went outside, to the **garden of Gethsemane**. For a while, **Jesus** went off on his own to pray, and it was when he came back to the **disciples** and started talking to them that an **angry mob** suddenly appeared, with **Judas** at its head. **He** walked straight up to **Jesus** and said, 'Hello, Teacher.' Suddenly, some of the **men** grabbed **Jesus**, arrested him and took him away.

The **disciples** were very frightened, and **they** all ran away—all except **Peter**, who followed the **mob**. **He** sat sadly by the **gate** of the high priest's palace. Inside, **he** could hear the **chief priests** holding a trial. All night, **people** came and went, telling lies about Jesus, while the priests tried to find evidence to kill him. Finally, just before dawn, **two men** came forward and said, 'We heard him say that he would pull down the temple and build it again in three days.'

'Are you the Messiah?' **Peter** heard one of the **priests** ask.

'Yes, I am,' he heard **Jesus** answer.

That was enough for the **priests**. Nobody was allowed to claim that they were the Son of God.

So, the next day, **Jesus** was taken outside the city and crucified. As **he** died, the sky turned dark, there was an **earthquake**, and a **curtain** in the temple was torn in two.

'This man really was the Son of God,' said one of the **Roman guards**. But it was too late now, his **disciples** thought as they left, broken-hearted. Their teacher, their friend and the person they had thought was their Messiah was dead. It was all over.

WHOOSH

Follow up

Discussion

- Why is Passover an important festival for the Jewish people?
- Why did the Jewish leaders want Jesus dead?
- What do you think Jesus meant when he said he would tear down the temple and build it again in three days?

Activity

- On green paper, draw around your hand several times. Cut out the hand shapes to use as palm leaves.
- Roll a piece of brown paper into a tube and glue the edge down. Stick the hand cut-outs on to the tube to make a palm branch.

Prayer

Thank you, Jesus, that you died so that I could be forgiven for all the wrong things I have done. Amen

36

Jesus is risen

MATTHEW 27:57—28:20; MARK 15:42—16:19; LUKE 23:50—24:53; JOHN 19:38—21:25

characters	objects	sounds
friends family disciples Joseph of Arimathea Pontius Pilate captain of the guard two women chief priests guards angel Jesus disciples Peter two people	tomb women's home earth shaking shafts of light house locked doors Lake Galilee	

Jesus' **friends**, his **family** and his **disciples** were heartbroken. Their teacher, their friend and their Saviour was dead. It was all over. They had followed him and trusted him, and **they** agreed that they hadn't really understood when he'd told them that he was going to die. But it had happened, just as he had said it would.

Later in the afternoon, **Joseph**, a wealthy man from Arimathea, visited **Pontius Pilate**, the governor of Judea, to ask for Jesus' body. **Pilate** sent for the **captain** of his guard to make sure that Jesus was actually dead, then **he** gave permission for **Joseph** to bury the body.

So **Joseph** wrapped the body in linen, added spices, and put Jesus in a new tomb that had just been cut into the rock. **Two** of the women who had been there when Jesus died followed **Joseph** and watched as **he** rolled a large stone across the opening. Then **they** went **home**.

WHOOSH

The **chief priests**, however, weren't quite ready to go home. They paid **Pilate** a visit.

'Sir,' **they** reminded him, 'that liar said that he would be raised up in three days. Suppose the disciples come and steal his body and tell everyone that he rose from the dead?'

But **Pilate** wasn't interested.

'You have a guard,' **he** answered. 'You'll have to do the best you can with that.' So the **chief priests** went to the tomb, sealed the stone and posted **guards**.

WHOOSH

The next day was the sabbath, and **everyone** stayed at **home**. Many **people** were weeping and mourning the death of their teacher and friend. But as soon as dawn broke on Sunday morning, the **women** went back to the **tomb** with spices, to get the body ready for a proper burial.

'How will we move that huge stone?' **Mary** wondered. But when **they** got there, the stone had already been rolled back. The **women** walked into the **tomb** and stopped in distress. The body had gone. Suddenly, **the earth** rocked under their feet and **shafts of light** blazed out as an **angel** appeared in front of them. **They** stopped being distressed. **They** started feeling very frightened. What was going on?

WHOOSH

'Why are you looking for a body?' the **angel** asked them. 'Jesus isn't here. He's risen. Don't you remember him telling you that this would happen?'

They were about to rush back to the disciples when, 'Good morning,' a **voice** said suddenly. And there he was—**Jesus**, alive again. **They** fell on their knees and worshipped him, full of joy.

'Go and tell the disciples to meet me in Galilee,' **he** told them. **They** ran, as fast as they possibly could, back to the **house** where the disciples were staying.

WHOOSH

'We've seen the Master!' **they** shouted to the **disciples** in excitement when they got back. 'He's alive, just like he said.' Sadly, **nobody** believed them and they all stayed where they were—all, that is, except **Peter**, who ran as fast as he could to the tomb. When **he** found it empty, **he** walked away, shaking his head.

And Peter wasn't the only one with a problem. The **guards** had fled into the city when the **angel** rolled the stone away. **They** were in real trouble now, but the **chief priests** soon came up with a plan. **They** gave the **guards** a lot of money to say that they had fallen asleep and the disciples had stolen the body.

WHOOSH

Later that day, **Jesus** suddenly appeared beside **two people** out walking.

'What's happened?' **he** asked, seeing their sad faces. **He** walked with them for a while, and **their** tears soon turned to joy when they realised who he was. **They** rushed back into Jerusalem.

'It's true! It's true!' they told the **disciples**. 'He's alive. We've seen him.'

But still the **disciples** didn't believe. It wasn't until **they** were eating supper that evening, with the **doors** securely locked because they were afraid of being arrested themselves, that **Jesus** came to see them.

'Peace to you,' **he** said. 'Why didn't you believe that I was alive?'

And then, finally, the **disciples** believed that he was really alive, and they did as they were told and went to **Galilee**.

WHOOSH

It was a very special time. The **disciples** went fishing again, just like they used to. One morning, **Jesus** lit a fire and cooked breakfast for them on the beach. **He** talked to them about what **he** wanted them to do. **He** explained that **they** were to go into the whole world and tell everyone the good news about God's kingdom. **He** told them that **he** was going to leave them, because it was time for him to go back to heaven.

But **he** also made them a very special promise—one that is still ours today.

'I will be with you, every day, until the end of time.'

WHOOSH

Follow up

Discussion

- Why didn't the disciples believe the women when they said that Jesus was alive?
- The chief priests told the guards to lie about the body. What was the problem with this lie?
- Why do you think Jesus wanted to spend time alone with his disciples in Galilee?

Activity

- Cut a circle of card in half. In one half, cut a D shape to make the tomb opening. Glue the long edges of the halves together.
- Cut a circle of card to be the stone and glue it to the empty tomb. Decorate the tomb with the words 'He is risen'.

Prayer

Jesus, thank you that you rose again and that before you returned to heaven you gave us a special promise—that you would be with us until the end of time. Amen

New Testament: stories Jesus told

Love your neighbour as much as you love yourself

37

The good Samaritan

LUKE 10:25–37

characters	objects	sounds
Jesus people lawyer man robbers priest Levite Samaritan innkeeper	Jerusalem Jericho donkey inn	

Wherever **Jesus** went, **people** would always follow him. **They** loved to hear him talking. He made it much easier to understand about God than the Pharisees and experts in the law did, who taught them in the temple. And when **Jesus** was talking to people, **they** often asked him questions. One day, **one** of the experts in law stood up with a question to test him.

'What do I need to do to get eternal life?' **he** asked.

'What is written in the law?' **Jesus** asked him. 'What do you think it says?' The lawyer knew all about the law, the rules that God had given to Moses, so **he** was quick with his answer.

'Love the Lord your God with all of your soul and all of your mind, and love your neighbour as much as you love yourself,' **he** said.

'That's a good answer,' **Jesus** smiled. 'Now go and do it and you will have eternal life.'

Hoping to show off his knowledge a little bit more, the **lawyer** said, 'Ah, but who *is* my neighbour?'

And this time, **Jesus** answered him by telling a story.

WHOOSH

The **crowd** settled down to listen. **They** loved a good story, and they loved listening to Jesus' stories in particular.

'Once upon a time, there was a **man** travelling from **Jerusalem** to **Jericho**. While **he** was walking along, **he** was attacked by **robbers**. **They** beat **him** up, **they** went through all his things and **they** took everything he had. **They** even took his clothes. Then **they** ran off and left the man with nothing, lying by the side of the road, nearly dead.'

The people in the **crowd** looked at each other and nodded. That was a really dangerous road to be walking along. It took most of the day to walk from **Jerusalem** to **Jericho**, and people were often beaten up and mugged there. In fact, some lonely parts of the road were so dangerous that **people** usually travelled along it in groups.

'But a **priest** who happened to be walking on the same road soon came along,' the story continued.

Everyone sat up a little and looked hopeful. Maybe the poor **man** was going to be saved after all. But then they heard **Jesus** saying, 'But **he** crossed over the road and carried on walking, straight past the man.'

Of course, **they** nodded to each other. A **priest** wouldn't be able to touch a man covered in blood. The law said that if he did, he would be unclean and he would have to wash himself in a special way so that he was clean again. A **priest** would keep the rules. So the **man** was left lying by the side of the road, nearly dead. What would happen to him?

WHOOSH

All sorts of people walked along the road—particularly priests and their helpers who had been working in the temple in Jerusalem. Perhaps someone else would come along.

'Next, a **Levite** came into sight,' **Jesus** continued. 'But **he** walked by on the other side of the road, too.'

'Well, of course he would,' **people** in the crowd muttered to each other. A Levite was a priest's helper. **He** knew the law. **He** wouldn't touch a body with blood on it. The priest and the Levite had to keep the law. If they didn't, there would be consequences. But that poor man! Wasn't anyone going to help him?

WHOOSH

'A while later, a **Samaritan** passed that way, riding on his **donkey**,' the story continued.

People looked at each other in shock. A Samaritan? But the Jews and the Samaritans hated each other. Surely the Samaritan wasn't going to help. No, this was another person who would just keep going.

'And when **he** saw the body lying by the side of the road,' the story went on, '**he** felt very sorry for the man. **He** stopped, got off his **donkey** and **went** over to see if **he** could help. **He** poured some oil and some wine on to the wounds, then **he** got some strips of cloth and bandaged up the **man** as best he could. Then, **lifting** the man on to his own **donkey, he** walked with him to the nearest **inn**, where **he** could take care of the man properly. The next day, when **he** needed to get on his way, the **Samaritan** gave the **innkeeper** two silver coins. "Look after him," **he** said, "and if it costs you any more than this, I'll call in on my return journey and pay you back." And with that, **he** left.'

People turned to each other, looking surprised. A Samaritan had helped a Jew!

'So,' **Jesus** said, turning to the **lawyer** who had asked who his neighbour was, 'of these three people in the story, which one do you think was the neighbour to the man who was mugged?'

'The one who took pity on him and cared for him,' the **lawyer** answered.

'Then you go and do the same,' said **Jesus**.

As **Jesus** got ready to go on his way, the **crowd** started to thin out. **People** walked away in groups, discussing what Jesus had just told them. Were they good neighbours?

WHOOSH

Follow up

Discussion

- Who is my neighbour?
- What did Jesus want the crowd to understand?
- In what ways can we help others?
- How can we love God with all of our soul and all of our mind?

Activity

On a bandage or thin strip of cloth, draw pictures or write sentences showing the different ways that we can help others and the ways that we can love God with all of our soul and all of our mind.

Prayer

Father, please help me to care for others, whoever they are. Thank you for the people who care for me. Amen

38

The lost son

LUKE 15:11–32

characters	objects	sounds
Jesus	property	music
a crowd	another country	snorting pigs
teachers and Pharisees	tables of food	
man/father	parties with dancing	
two sons	dying crops	
friends	dying animals	
servants	farms	
farmers	pigs	
	nice home	
	feast	

Wherever **Jesus** went, **crowds** of people followed him. **They** loved to listen to his stories. Often, though, there were people there who moaned, and today was no exception. As the **crowd** gathered around so that they could hear what **Jesus** said, some of the **teachers** and **Pharisees** standing nearby started **grumbling** to each other. 'He's friendly with bad people,' **they** complained, rolling their eyes and shrugging their shoulders. 'Do you know, he even has meals with them!'

But nobody was really listening to them. **People** wanted to listen to a good story, not a bunch of moaning minnies. 'Shhh,' the **crowd** hushed them. 'Listen!'

WHOOSH

There was once a **man** with **two sons**, the story started. The **crowd** settled down. That could be a story about any one of them.

The **younger son** was a bit selfish. Instead of waiting for his father to die, **he** asked his **father** if he could have his share of the money straight away. Sadly, his **father** decided to give him what he wanted and, soon afterwards, bored and looking for a good time, **the son** packed his bags and **moved** to another country where nobody could tell him what to do. **He** had a great time—**tables** full of **good food**, the best clothes, loads of **friends**. There was **music, dancing** and wild **parties. He** was very happy.

But then, one day, **he** ran out of money. Then the **crops** died. **Animals** started to die of hunger. There wasn't enough food to eat and suddenly all his **friends** disappeared. No parties, no friends and not enough to eat. Instead of being very rich and very popular, **he** was suddenly very lonely and very, very hungry.

WHOOSH

The **younger son** had been used to having the best of everything brought to him by **servants**, but those days were over. **He** would have to find a job or **he** would starve to death. **He** was already getting very thin. So **he** tramped from **farm** to **farm**, **asking** for work and getting hungrier and hungrier. The **farmers** didn't have enough food for themselves and their families, so they weren't about to give any to a tramp.

But then one day, when he was running out of hope, a **farmer** offered him a job. Grateful for anything, he agreed to look after the man's **pigs**. It was a disgusting job. According to the rules of his religion, **he** couldn't even touch pigs, let alone **muck** them out and **feed** them. But **he** was desperate and at least **he** could eat the pigswill.

WHOOSH

One day, while the **son** was sitting with the **pigs**, listening to them **snorting**, **he** started thinking about his **father**. He thought about the **nice home** he had left. He thought about the **servants** and, most of all, he thought about the good **food** that the **servants** cooked. He could almost smell it! And while **he** was thinking, he wondered why **he** was being so silly, **eating** pig food when he could be at **home**. **He** decided to go **home** and ask if he could be a servant. 'I'm not good enough to be his son any more, but I could be a worker,' **he** thought. So **he** set off **home**.

As **he** got near, **he** practised what he was going to say to his dad: 'I've sinned against God and you. I'm sorry.'

WHOOSH

But the **son** didn't have time to say anything. **He** was still a long way from **home** when he saw his father rushing towards **him**, **his** arms open wide in welcome. His **father** called to the **servants** to bring the best clothes and sandals for **his son**. **He** put a ring on his finger. **He** told the servants to get a huge **feast** ready and **they** all had a great **party**.

The **older son** wasn't too pleased when he got home. **He** called one of the servants to **ask him** what was going on. When **he** found out that it was a party for his brother, **he** got so mad and jealous that he wouldn't even go into the **house**.

When his **father** came out to plead with him, **he** whinged about his little brother wasting all the money while he, the older son, slaved away. His **father** pointed to the land and the house. 'All of this is yours,' **he** said, 'but your brother was dead and now he's alive. Be glad. Celebrate.'

And without another word, the **father** rushed back into the **house**. His son had been lost. But now he was found.

WHOOSH

Follow up

Discussion

- In advance, ask your children to discover how their families prepared for their arrival. How was their name chosen? What special arrangements were made for them? Who came to visit them when they were born? Do they have a favourite toy from their early childhood? You might like to have similar information ready about yourself.
- Invite children to share their stories. Every child will have personal information which, together with their last name, identifies them as belonging to a family. It also demonstrates how much the people in their family love them (by choosing a name, getting ready, buying clothes and toys, visiting them and so on).
- Draw the parallel with God's family, to which he invites us to belong. Our human families help us to understand just how much God loves us. They love us and forgive us, even when we do things that upset them. And when we let God down, we are still part of his family, too.

Prayer

Thank you, God, that you love everyone in your family and that I can be part of it. Thank you that, no matter what I do, you will still love me and I can still belong. Amen

39

The lost sheep

MATTHEW 18:12–14; LUKE 15:1–10; JOHN 10:11–15

characters	objects	sounds
people Jesus Pharisees teachers of the law children shepherd friends and neighbours woman	sheep wild animals rocks brambles bushes home	murmur

All sorts of **people** were crowding around **Jesus**, wanting to listen to him speak. As usual, the **Pharisees** and the **teachers of the law** were there, keeping an eye on him and waiting for an opportunity to catch him out with a tricky question or two.

'Look at him,' one of the **Pharisees** grumbled. 'He welcomes sinners and tax collectors. Apparently, he even eats with them,' **he** carried on, looking around at his **friends** in a very superior manner. **They** all smiled at each other: **they** weren't like this man Jesus that everybody followed around. Nobody could accuse them of spending time with people who didn't keep the law to the very letter. **They** were careful who they were seen with. It was the outside of you that mattered, after all. You needed to be seen doing the right thing.

WHOOSH

Jesus called one of the **children** from the **crowd** to come and stand with him.

'Unless you change and become like a little child,' **he** told the crowd, smiling at the **child**, 'you will never enter God's kingdom.'

'Hmph!' said one of the **Pharisees**. 'Behave like a child? What will he say next?'

'Well, suppose...' **Jesus** started to say. The **crowd** sensed a story coming, and as **they** settled down to listen, a hush fell over them. The **Pharisees** stood at a safe distance, still looking superior.

'Suppose you were a shepherd,' **Jesus** finished the sentence. Yes, **they** could imagine that. **They** knew plenty of shepherds.

'Suppose you were a **shepherd** with a hundred **sheep**. **You** care for them. When **wild animals** attack, you don't run away like a paid helper would. **You** defend your **sheep**. You would even die for them. **You** watch over them and keep them safe, because sometimes they can do silly things.

'Then, one day, when **you** count your **sheep**, **you** only count 99. **You** count again, just in case you missed one... 97, 98, 99. No, there's definitely one missing. What do you do?' **Jesus** asked. 'Do **you** sit and wait until the sheep reappears on its own? No, of course you don't. **You** leave the 99 **sheep** that are safe and well, while **you** go and look for the lost one.'

Everyone nodded their agreement. Shepherds often had to leave their sheep with each other to go and hunt for one that had got lost.

WHOOSH

'**You** look everywhere,' **Jesus** said. 'And **you** keep looking until you find it. **You** hunt behind **rocks**. You search in the **brambles** and the **bushes**. And when **you** finally find it, **you** put the **sheep** up on your shoulders and go back to the rest of your flock. When **you** get **home**, you call on all your **friends** and **neighbours** and say, "Come and celebrate with me. I've found my lost sheep."'

Everyone looked at each other and smiled in agreement. That was exactly what they would do.

'Or suppose...' **Jesus** continued, to the delight of the crowd, who sensed another story coming. 'Suppose a **woman** has ten silver coins and she loses one.'

A sympathetic **murmur** went around the crowd. All the married **women** knew exactly how they had felt when they were brides and wore their silver coins. **They** would have been devastated to lose one.

Jesus carried on, 'Wouldn't **she** light a lamp straight away and sweep every single corner of her house? Wouldn't **she** search every nook and cranny until she found it? And when **she** found it, **she** would call her neighbours and invite them to celebrate with her, because what was lost had been found.'

WHOOSH

Everyone looked intently at **Jesus** as he finished what he was saying. **They** all knew someone who had lost something they valued, even if they hadn't lost anything themselves.

'I'm telling you,' **Jesus** concluded, 'my Father in heaven celebrates in just the same way when someone who has sinned says they are truly sorry.'

What did it mean? **people** pondered as they sat there. Were they among the sinners? And why was Jesus telling them this story? Only the **Pharisees** looked pleased with themselves. **They** knew they were like the 99 sheep who didn't need to be found. They had nothing to be sorry for.

It wasn't long before **people** understood what Jesus meant. 'I am the good shepherd,' **he** told them when he was talking to them on another day. **He** told them that he was like the shepherd who would never run away when wild animals attacked.

'I know my sheep and they know my voice,' **he** said. 'I am the good shepherd, and I will give up my life for my sheep. I am like the gate of the sheepfold. People who come in through me will be saved.'

On that occasion, **lots of people** walked away, saying, 'He must be mad,' but **some** of the crowd understood what he meant. **They** knew they were like the lost sheep that needed to be found.

WHOOSH

Follow up

Discussion

- Has anyone been lost? What did the adults do?
- Has anyone ever lost something? What did they do?
- Why did Jesus tell this story?
- Why is God so happy when someone chooses to follow him?

Activity

- Draw a shepherd in one corner of a piece of A4 paper. Draw a sheep in the opposite corner. Create a maze by drawing wavy, tangled lines around the page. Only one line should touch both the shepherd and the sheep. Add some rocks, brambles and bushes in the spaces between the lines.
- Challenge friends to find your lost sheep.

Prayer

Father, thank you that you love me so much that you sent Jesus so that I could have eternal life. Thank you that you will never stop loving me. Amen

40

Building work

MATTHEW 7:24–29; LUKE 6:47–49; 12:15–21; 14:28–33

characters	objects	sounds
Jesus	barns	barns being demolished
crowds	tower	building barns
young man	house built on rock	laughter
rich farmer	door	storm
workers	windows	howling wind
God	rain	lashing rain
people	rivers	rattling and creaking
two men	flooded land	crash
	house built on sand	

One day, **Jesus** was talking to the **crowds** of people who always followed him everywhere he went. **They** loved to ask him questions, and often he would answer a question by telling a story. Today was no different.

'Tell my brother to give me my share of the money that my father left when he died,' one cross **young man** called out.

'Don't be greedy,' **Jesus** said in answer, looking round at everyone. 'Your value as a person doesn't depend on what you own.'

And then **he** told a story.

Once there was a **man** who owned a farm. **He** was very successful and very rich. One year, when his **workers** had finished the harvest, **he** discovered that the crops that year had done so well that he didn't have enough room in his **barns** to store all the grain.

'I know what I'll do,' **he** thought to himself. And **he** got his **workers** to **pull down** all the **barns** that he owned and **build** bigger **barns** so that all the grain could be stored. **He** was rather pleased with this idea. Eventually, **he** would have such big barns, and so much money, that he wouldn't need to work any more. **He** could just party and enjoy himself.

But **God** said to him, 'You fool. You are going to die tonight. What use will bigger barns be to you then? Who will get all your money?'

'That,' said **Jesus** in conclusion, 'is what happens to people who save everything up for themselves. They are rich in their own eyes, but very poor in God's eyes.'

WHOOSH

Another time, **Jesus** was walking, and the **crowds** just walked along with him. Suddenly **he** turned to them and said, 'You can't really follow me, you know, unless you love me more than you love your own life.' And **he** went on to explain what he meant by telling another story.

Suppose **you** decide one day that you want to build a **tower**. Do **you** just go out, find some land and start building? Of course not. **You** draw up plans. **You** sit down and work out how much it's going to cost. **You** check to see if you have enough money to build it. If you start building before you've done all of this, then you might not be able to finish. Then **people** will see what is happening and they will **laugh** at you. **They** will say, 'Look, he started building a tower without knowing whether he could finish it.'

'If you want to follow me,' said **Jesus**, 'you need to be sure that you want to pay what it will cost you.'

WHOOSH

And then on another day, **Jesus** wanted to explain to the **crowd** what it meant to listen to what he was saying and to obey it. **He** told them a story about **two men** who each wanted to build themselves a new house.

The **first man** did some surveys before he chose a good piece of land for a building. **He** knew that there was **rock** underneath the soil, which would be a good, firm foundation for his house. **He** started to build. Every day, **he** watched his **house** get a little bit bigger, and a little bit bigger, until one day **it** was finished and **he** was able to move in. It was a lovely **house** and he was very proud of it.

A few days later, there was a terrible **storm**. **Rain** lashed against the **building**. **Wind** beat against the **door** and howled through the **windows**. Everything **rattled** and **creaked**. And the **rain** just carried on pouring down until eventually the **rivers** broke their banks and the **land flooded**.

But inside his **house, the man** knew that he was safe, because he had built his **house** on solid rock.

WHOOSH

The **second man** was in a hurry to get his house finished. **He** chose a nice plot of land with good views and started building. Just like the first man, **he** watched his **house** get a little bit bigger, and a little bit bigger, and soon **it** was finished. **He** moved in to his beautiful new **house**. **He** was very pleased with it.

His house was battered by the **storm**, too. **Rain** lashed against his building. **Wind** beat against his **door** and **howled** through his **windows**. Everything **rattled** and **creaked**, just like the first man's house. And the **rain** just carried on pouring down until the **rivers** burst their banks and the **land flooded**.

But inside his **house**, the **second man** was getting scared. His **house** was starting to move. **It** was starting to **lean**. And then **it** was washed away in the flood, falling with an almighty great **crash**. His house wasn't safe, because he had built it on sand.

'And so,' finished **Jesus**, 'if you hear and obey what I say, you will be like the first man, building on solid rock. If you don't listen and obey, you will be foolish, just like the man who built on sand.'

The **crowds** were amazed when he finished telling the story. This was very different from the teaching that they were given by the teachers in the temple!

WHOOSH

Follow up

Discussion

- What did Jesus want people to understand from these stories?
- What does it mean to build our lives on solid rock?
- What sort of people will we be?

Activity

Take a large stone and paint a house on it. Remember to build your life on solid rock!

Prayer

Father, please help me to build my life on solid rock. Help me to understand what that means day by day. Amen

41

The sower

MATTHEW 13:1–23

characters	objects	sounds
Jesus	house	
crowd	road	
farmer	birds	
disciples	stony ground	
people who hear	sun	
people who listen	little shoots	
people who are determined to get rich	plants	
people who obey God	thorn bushes	
people sowing thistles	strong plants	
workers	thistles	
woman	tiny shoots	
	barn	
	mustard seed	
	tree	
	field	

One day, **Jesus** left the **house** to sit by the shore of Lake Galilee. It wasn't long before a **crowd** gathered, and soon there were so many people that **Jesus** decided to sit in a boat on the lake and talk to people from there. It was a day for telling stories.

A **farmer** went out into his fields to sow seed. **He** scooped up the seed in handfuls and threw it out on to the ground that he had prepared. As **he** threw it, some of the seed fell on the **road**. **Birds** came along behind the **farmer**, pecking it up. Some of it fell on to **stony ground** where the soil was thin. **It** started to grow, but when the **sun** came up, the **little shoots** got scorched and they dried up and died, because the roots weren't strong enough to find water. Some seed fell on to ground where **thorn bushes** grew, and although the **plants** started to grow, they were soon choked by the **bushes**. And some of the seed fell on the good, rich soil that the farmer had prepared. **It** grew into **strong plants** and produced lots of grain for the farmer.

'If you've got ears, make sure you listen!' **Jesus** told them.

WHOOSH

'Why do you tell people stories?' the **disciples** asked **Jesus**.

Jesus explained that he was trying to get people to understand what God's kingdom was like. The trouble was, **people** heard but didn't listen. **They** looked, but they didn't see.

'**People** are stubborn,' **Jesus** said. 'They don't want to listen to what I'm saying. Not like you—you are really eager to see and listen.' Then **he** explained the story he had just told.

The seed that fell on the road is like the **people who hear** about the kingdom of God, but **they** don't take time really to listen and understand it. Then life crowds in and pushes what they have heard out of their minds. The seed that fell on the stony ground is like the **people who listen** and understand, but because **they** don't take time to develop deep roots, when the going gets tough **they** just give up really quickly.

The seeds that fell in the thorn bushes are like the **people who are determined to get rich**, and **they** are more concerned about what **they** need than about following God. And the good seed is like the **people** who listen, who understand, and **who are determined to obey God**.

WHOOSH

Then **Jesus** went on to tell the crowd another story. It was a day for stories!

The kingdom of God is like a **farmer** who **buys** some really good wheat seed and **sows** it in his field. But then, while **he's** asleep one night, **people** come into the field and **sow** thistles as well. For a while, nothing is different, but then one day his **workers** notice that **thistles** are mixed in with the **tiny shoots** from the good seed.

'Sir,' **they** say to the **farmer**, 'you planted good seed. Where have these thistles come from? Shall we pull them up?'

'An enemy did this,' **he** answers. 'No, leave the thistles. If you pull them up now, you will pull up the plants as well.' So **they** wait until the harvest, then **his workers** sort the good plants from the thistles. The **thistles** are bundled up and burnt, but the wheat is stored in the **barn**.

WHOOSH

The kingdom of God is like a **farmer**. **He** plants a tiny little **mustard seed** in his field. Although it is the tiniest little seed possible, **it** shoots, and then **it** grows, and eventually **it** becomes a **tree**. Even birds perch and build nests in its branches—and all from one tiny little seed.

Or the kingdom of God is like a **woman** making bread. **She** weighs out her flour, then **she** adds yeast to it, then **she** kneads the dough and **leaves** it for a while. The dough rises, because the yeast has worked its way through all of the flour.

And then **Jesus** got out of the boat and went back into the **house**. His **disciples** went with him.

'What did you mean by the story of the weeds?' **they** asked him.

WHOOSH

So **Jesus** explained the story to his **disciples**. The **farmer** scattering the seed was like him. The **field** where the seed was sowed was the world. The **good seeds** were the **people** who choose to belong to the kingdom of God, but the **thistles** were **those** who choose not to follow God. The **people** scattering the thistles were like the devil. The harvest was the end of time and the **workers** who collect the harvest were God's angels.

'That's how it will be at the end of time,' **Jesus** said. 'My angels will separate those who have chosen to belong to the kingdom of God and those who have chosen not to. Those who belong will shine like the sun in the kingdom of God.

'So if you have ears,' **Jesus** concluded, 'make sure you really listen!'

WHOOSH

Follow up

Discussion

- What is the difference between hearing and listening?
- How do we hear about God's kingdom?
- What different choices can we make when we hear about God?
- How do Jesus' stories help us to understand?

Activity

- Take a soaked broad bean seed, some damp kitchen roll and a glass jar.
- Place the bean on the kitchen roll inside the jar. Water it daily with a small amount of water. Watch the roots, then the shoots, grow.

Prayer

Father, thank you for the people who tell me about you. Help me to listen and to understand.
Amen

42

Planning ahead

MATTHEW 25:1–30

characters	objects	sounds
Jesus disciples ten girls someone shouting bridegroom man/master three servants angels people who are hungry, thirsty, sick, without clothes strangers	house wedding door	

Sometimes **Jesus** spent time with just his **disciples**, and **they** often had questions to ask him. One day **they** asked him what it would be like at the end of time, and **Jesus** told them two stories.

Once, there were **ten girls** who were going to be bridesmaids at a wedding. **They** needed to be ready to meet the bridegroom and take him to the **house** where the wedding was being held. Off the **ten girls** went to wait for the bridegroom, **taking** their oil lamps with them, ready for when it got dark. **Five** of the girls were sensible, and **they** took extra oil with their lamps. But **five** of the girls were foolish, and **they** didn't bother with extra oil.

They waited, and **they** waited, but the groom didn't arrive. **They** started to feel sleepy, and eventually **they** all fell asleep.

WHOOSH

The **ten girls** hadn't been asleep long when **someone** started shouting, 'Here he is! Let's go and meet him.' And there was the **groom**, arriving in the middle of the night. **The girls** got up quickly and lit their lamps, but the **foolish girls** soon found that their lamps went out.

'Quickly,' **they** said, 'give us some of your oil.' But the **sensible girls** wouldn't part with their oil, because **they** knew they would soon need it themselves.

So off the **foolish girls** went to buy some more oil. While **they** were gone, the **bridegroom** arrived, and by the time **they** got back, the **wedding** had started and the **door** was locked.

'Always be ready,' **Jesus** told his **disciples**. 'You never know when the end of time will happen.'

WHOOSH

But then **Jesus** continued. **He** told them, The end of time is also like a **man** who had to go away for a while. **The man** decided that he would leave **three** of his **servants** in charge of everything he owned while he was gone. **He** knew what each servant was capable of doing, so when **he** called the **first servant**, he gave him five thousand coins. Then **he** called his **second servant** and gave **him** two thousand coins. And to the **third servant he** gave just one thousand coins. Then **he** left the country.

As soon as their **master** had left, the **servants** started to think about what to do with the money. The **first servant** worked hard with his five thousand coins and **he** managed to earn another five thousand. The **second servant** worked hard, too, and **he** also doubled the money that he had been given. But the **third servant** decided not to do any work. Instead, **he** went outside, **dug** a hole, **put** the coins in the hole and **covered** them over.

WHOOSH

Some time later, the **master** of the house returned from his journey. **He** called his **servants** to see him, because **he** wanted to know what they had done with the money that he had given them.

The **first servant** brought in the five thousand coins that **he** had been given and proudly handed over another bag of money. 'Sir,' **he** said, 'you gave me five thousand and I earned another five thousand.'

'Wonderful,' the **master** said. 'What a good servant. I put you in charge of a little, and you have worked hard, so now **I will** put you in charge of much more.'

Then the **second servant** came in and handed over not just the two thousand coins that **he** had been given, but another two thousand to go with them.

'Wonderful,' said the **master** again. 'What a good and faithful servant you are.' And **he** was also given much more to look after.

WHOOSH

But then the **third servant** came in. **On** hearing about the master's return, **he** had rushed outside and **dug** up the buried coins. When **he** went to see his **master, he** handed over the coins and **said,** 'I was frightened, because I know that you are hard to get on with. So I buried your money, and here it is.'

The **master** was angry. 'You lazy good-for-nothing,' **he** said. 'So I'm hard to get on with, am I? The very least you could have done would have been to put it in the bank, so that I got some interest on the money while I was gone.' And then **he** sent his **worthless servant** away.

WHOOSH

One day, **Jesus** explained to the **disciples, I** will come with all my **angels** to sort **people** out. **Those** who are part of God's kingdom will be welcomed by my Father, but **those** who are not part of God's kingdom will be sent away from him for ever.

Because even though God isn't actually here, if **you** feed **someone** who is hungry, or give **someone** a drink when they're thirsty, or welcome **someone** who is a stranger, or give clothes to **people** who have none, or **care** for someone when they're sick, then it's just the same as if **you** did those things for God himself. People who do these things will spend eternity with God.

WHOOSH

Follow up

Discussion

- What was Jesus trying to explain in these stories?
- How does Jesus say that we can show our love for God?
- How can we know what gifts God has given us?

Activity

- Take it in turns to spin a bottle. The spinner must say something positive about the person to whom the bottle points when it stops spinning. Ensure that everyone has a go.
- How can we use the gifts that have been identified in us to show God's love to other people this week?

Prayer

Thank you, Father, for giving me gifts. Help me to use them for other people so that I can show them your love. Amen

New Testament: people Jesus met

43

Special friends

MATTHEW 4:18–22; 9:9–13; MARK 1:16–20; 3:13–19; LUKE 5:1–11, 27–31; 6:12–16; JOHN 1:35–49

characters	objects	sounds
Jesus	River Jordan	
John the Baptist	prison	
crowds	fishing boats	
fishermen	nets	
Simon Peter	fish	
Andrew	tax collector's booth	
friends	Matthew's house	
James	mountains	
John		
Zebedee		
Philip		
Nathaniel		
Matthew		
people		
Pharisees		

When **Jesus** was about 30 years old, **he** knew that it was time for him to start the work that he had come to earth to do—telling people about the kingdom of God. His cousin, **John the Baptist**, was already drawing **crowds** of people, telling them how he was preparing the way for someone to come and save them from their sins. This was their Messiah, their Saviour, the person that God had promised to send to save them.

When **people** were sorry for the things **they** had done wrong, **John** baptised them in the **River Jordan**. Even **Jesus** himself had been baptised. But then **John** was arrested and put in **prison**, and **Jesus** knew that he had to go back to Galilee and start telling people the good news.

WHOOSH

'This is good news,' **Jesus** told **people** who came to listen to him speak. 'God's kingdom is coming. Turn back to God.' Everywhere **he** went, **people** crowded to hear him speak. But **Jesus** knew that he needed to train other people to share the good news.

One day, while **Jesus** was walking along the beach of Lake Galilee, **he** stopped to watch the **fishermen** working. **They** had been out fishing overnight, and now **they** had tied up their **boats** and were washing their nets. The **crowds** were starting to build up again, so **Jesus** called to one of the **fishermen** to ask if he could get into the **boat**.

'Row it out a little way from the shore,' **he** said, and then **he** sat in the **boat** and talked to the **people** from there.

WHOOSH

When **Jesus** had finished talking, he turned to **Simon Peter**, the fisherman who had rowed him out on to the lake, and asked **him** to **row** into deeper water. Then **he** told **Simon** to let the **nets** down and catch some fish.

'I will,' said **Simon**, 'since you've asked me to, but we've been fishing all night and caught nothing.' But when **he** let the **nets** down, **he** caught so many **fish** that the **nets** were in danger of ripping apart. **Simon** waved to his **friends** in another **boat** to come and help them. With some heaving and pulling, **they** managed to empty the nets into both **boats**, but there were so many **fish** that the **boats** nearly sank.

Everyone was amazed as they finally managed to haul the heavy **boats** up on to the beach.

'We've found the Messiah,' said **Andrew**, Simon's brother, when they had unloaded the fish.

'Don't be afraid,' **Jesus** said to **Simon**. 'I want you to follow me and bring in people instead of fish.'

WHOOSH

Straight away, without a second thought, **Andrew** and **Simon Peter** tied up their **boat**, left everything and followed **Jesus**. As **they** walked along the beach together, Jesus stopped to watch **James** and **John** fishing. They were brothers, too, and they had seen everything that happened when Simon Peter and Andrew threw out their nets. **They** were sitting in a boat with their father, **Zebedee**, checking their nets and getting them ready to throw out. But when **Jesus** called them, **they** got out of the boat, left everything and followed him.

WHOOSH

The next day, **Jesus** was walking on the beach of Lake Galilee again when **he** met **Philip**. Again Jesus said, 'Come and follow me.' And straight away, **Philip** rushed off to find his brother, **Nathaniel**. 'Come and meet the Messiah,' **he** said in great excitement. So **Nathaniel** went to meet Jesus, and **he** and **Philip** both decided to become followers.

Another day, **Jesus** was on his way home when he spotted **Matthew**, a tax collector, sitting at the **booth** where **people** had to go to pay their tax.

'Come with me,' **Jesus** invited him, and that's exactly what **Matthew** did. They went to Matthew's **house** together, and **Jesus** had a meal with him. The **Pharisees** sneered when they heard about it.

'Why does your teacher eat with sinners?' **they** asked the **people** who were waiting for Jesus. But **Jesus** heard them, and **he** answered by saying, 'Because I came to invite sinners to follow me, not good people.'

WHOOSH

Jesus had **many followers** by this time and it was difficult for him to find time away from the crowds who followed him everywhere he went. One night, **he** went off on his own into the **mountains** so that he could be alone to pray. **He** spent the night there, and the next morning **he** asked some of his **followers** to join him. From the group of followers, **he** chose **twelve men** to be his disciples. These were the **men he** was going to train to go out into the world and share the good news with everyone. These were the **men** who would **work** alongside **Jesus** for the next three years, **learning** from him and **growing** in their understanding of the kingdom of God.

WHOOSH

Follow up

Discussion

- What makes a good friend?
- What do you think Jesus was looking for in these friends?
- Does Jesus still invite people to be his friends today? If so, who are they?
- What different choices do people make about following Jesus?

Activity

- Draw a large outline of a person.
- Provide each child with a sticky note and ask them to write on the note one quality of a good friend. Invite the children to stick their notes on to the outline. Stick notes around the outside of the outline for external qualities, and inside for internal qualities.

Prayer

Father, please help me to be a good friend to other people, so that they can understand how much you love them. Amen

44

The wedding at Cana in Galilee

JOHN 2:1–11; 3:1–21

characters	objects	sounds
Jesus disciples Mary guests servants master of the feast bridegroom Jesus' brothers Nicodemus	wedding feast stone water jars Jerusalem	

Everywhere that Jesus went, he was followed by lots of people, because they loved to listen to him speak. To help him with his work, **Jesus** chose twelve **disciples** who were going to live with him, work with him and learn from him for the next three years. There was a lot that **he** needed to teach them in a very short time.

One day, **Jesus** and his **disciples** were invited to a **wedding feast**, along with Jesus' mother, **Mary**. The wedding was at a place called Cana, in Galilee. There was plenty to eat and drink and the **guests** were all enjoying the **feast** and celebrating the marriage of their friends. Until, that is, the wine ran out.

WHOOSH

Mary had heard about the wine running out from the **servants**, and she went to **Jesus**, to tell him.

'Why are you involving me?' **Jesus** asked **her**. But instead of answering the question he had asked, **Mary** just turned to the **servants** who were standing nearby and **said**, 'Do whatever he tells you to do.'

In the corner of the room there were **six** huge **stone water jars**. At the beginning of the feast they had all been full of water, ready for the **guests** to wash their hands before they ate. But they were empty now, and **Jesus** pointed to the stone jars.

'Fill them up with water,' **he** told the **servants**, 'right to the very top of each jar.'

The **servants** looked at one another in dismay. Didn't he understand that it was the wine that had run out? It was going to be very, very embarrassing for the bridegroom when all the guests found out what had happened. But Mary had told them to do whatever Jesus told them to do.

WHOOSH

There was nothing to lose by doing as Jesus had said, so, as quickly as they could, the **servants** filled each of the **jars** to the brim with water.

'Now take some of the water to the master of the feast,' **Jesus** told them when he saw that they had done as he asked. **They** exchanged worried glances as **they** drew out some of the water. The **servant** who had to take it to the **master** of the feast looked the most anxious of all, as the **master** lifted the cup of water to his lips.

'That's amazing,' said the **master**, as he went to find the **bridegroom**. 'Why would he do that?'

The **servants** all looked at each other again. What did he mean? Why would he do what?

The **master** of the feast called the **bridegroom** to one side and started talking to him. 'Why did you keep your best wine till last?' **he** asked the surprised **groom**. 'Usually, people give the best wine first at a wedding.' The **master** of the feast held out the cup. And sure enough, when the **bridegroom** tasted the wine, it was far better than anything that had been served so far.

Only the **servants** who had drawn the water in the jars really knew what had happened.

WHOOSH

The **disciples** were amazed. This was Jesus' first miracle, and it helped them to trust him. **They** talked about it as they walked back to Capernaum after the wedding feast. It was nearly time to go to Jerusalem to celebrate Passover, so **they** stayed with **Jesus**' mother and **brothers** for a few days before setting out for **Jerusalem**.

One night, while **they** were in **Jerusalem, Jesus** was visited by a man called **Nicodemus. He** was a Pharisee and a Jewish leader who had heard all about Jesus and wanted to know how to become part of the kingdom of God. **He** had come at night so that the other religious leaders wouldn't know what he was doing. But when **he** asked **Jesus** how to join the kingdom of God, **he** got a rather surprising answer.

WHOOSH

'If you want to be part of the kingdom of God, you have to be born again,' Jesus said.

Nicodemus frowned, feeling puzzled. How could he possibly be born again? He'd been born once and now he was grown up. Was he supposed to go back to being a baby again?

'I mean spiritually born again,' **Jesus** explained, seeing **Nicodemus**' puzzled look. **He** explained that the only way to God was through him, Jesus, the Son of God.

'God sent me into this world,' **he** said, 'because he wants everyone to share eternity with him.'

'What did it all mean?' wondered **Nicodemus** as **he** walked away. How could this man Jesus be the only way to God's kingdom? He was just Joseph's son from Nazareth. OK, he was respected as a teacher and lots of people followed him—but saving the world, just by getting people to believe in him? Was trusting Jesus really the way to spend eternity with God? Was he really who he said he was?

WHOOSH

Follow up

Discussion

- How do you think that Jesus' first miracle helped his disciples to trust him more?
- What did Jesus mean when he told Nicodemus that he would have to be born again?
- How did Jesus say that we could become part of God's kingdom?
- Jesus provided what people at the wedding feast needed. What things do we need that God provides for us?

Activity

- Give each child a large cut-out of a water jar, about A3 size, or invite them to draw and cut out their own jar.
- Write or draw on the jar the things that we need, that God provides for us.

Prayer

Thank you, Father, that we can be part of your kingdom and that we can spend eternity with you. Help me to think about what it means to follow you. Amen

45

Learning to trust

MATTHEW 8:23—9:8; MARK 4:35–41; LUKE 8:22–39

characters	objects	sounds
Jesus	fishing boat	splashing waves
crowds of people	wind	creaking mast
disciples	sails	howling wind
man	mountains	lashing rain
everyone	storm	crashing waves
group of friends	waves	creaking and groaning
teachers of the law	calm water	
paralysed man	gentle breeze	
	town	

Jesus had been at Lake Galilee all day, talking to **people** and telling them stories to try to explain about the kingdom of God. At one point, the crowds on the beach were so big that **Jesus** climbed into one of the **fishing boats** and spoke to them from there, with the **boat** bobbing on the water as the waves **splashed** against the wooden sides.

As evening came, **Jesus** was feeling very tired. Sometimes he liked to be alone with his disciples so that he could explain the stories he had been telling the crowds and answer their questions. So when **he** suggested that **they** should sail across to the other side of the lake, where it was quiet, **they** all agreed. **Pulling** in the oars and **hoisting** the sails, **Jesus** and his **disciples** set sail across the lake.

WHOOSH

As the **wind** filled the **sails**, the **disciples** looked around. Some of them knew this lake like the backs of their hands: they had sailed and fished on these waters since they were boys. **They** looked at the familiar **mountains** surrounding the water, and **they** thought about the sudden storms that could come out of nowhere. Tired out by a long day, **Jesus** had gone to the stern of the **boat** and fallen asleep on a cushion.

Suddenly, without any warning, one of those fierce **storms** blew up. The mast started to **creak** as the **wind howled** and the **rain lashed** down. Quickly, the **disciples** furled the **sails** and **four** of them started to row. But that soon proved useless, too. And even though **they** were experienced sailors, even though **they** had seen plenty of these sudden storms, and even though **they** knew exactly what to do, **they** were terrified. **They** had never seen anything this bad.

WHOOSH

As bigger and bigger **waves crashed** over the **boat, the disciples** looked at **Jesus**, still sleeping peacefully as if nothing was happening. The **boat** was being tossed around, **creaking** and **groaning** as if it would break up any minute. **Their** fear grew, until they couldn't bear it any longer.

'Jesus, Jesus!' **they** shouted as **they** shook him awake. 'We're going to drown. Don't you care?'

Jesus stood up in the **boat** and told the **wind** to stop blowing. Then **he** looked at the **waves**. 'Be quiet,' **he** told them. 'Be still.' And **everything** went quiet. The lake was calm and everything was peaceful again.

Turning to his **disciples**, **Jesus** said, 'Why are you so frightened? Do you have no faith?'

So then the **disciples** were even more terrified.

'Who is this man?' **they** asked each other. **They** looked at the **calm water**, which moments ago had been swamping the boat with its huge waves. **They** felt the **gentle breeze** on their faces as the **boat** moved across the water. Even the wind and the waves obeyed this man.

WHOOSH

Wherever he went, Jesus met someone who needed his help. No sooner had **he** reached the far side of the lake than he was met by a **man** who desperately needed healing of an illness. So **Jesus** healed him, and when it was time for **him** to get back into the boat to go home, the **man** pleaded to be allowed to go with him.

'No,' said **Jesus**. Instead, **he** sent the man back to his home **town** to tell people about how God had healed him. And that was exactly what **he** did. **He** told **everyone** he met about Jesus, and **people** were amazed that a man who had been so ill could be made completely well.

WHOOSH

Even after **Jesus and the disciples** had sailed back across the lake to go home, there was still a **crowd** waiting. Among the crowd was a **group of friends. They** had heard about Jesus healing people, and they had brought their **friend** to meet him. **The friend** couldn't walk, so they **had** carried him on a mat. As soon as **Jesus** saw the man, **he** said, 'Your sins are forgiven.'

The **teachers of the law** from the temple followed Jesus, too. They didn't want to learn from him; they wanted to try to catch him out. When **they** heard him say this, **they** muttered to each other, 'Only God can forgive sins. Who does he think he is?'

Knowing what **they** were thinking, **Jesus** turned to them and said, 'I have the authority to forgive sin.' Then **he** turned back to the **paralysed man** and told him to start walking. And that was exactly what the **man** did. **He** stood up, rolled up his mat and walked home with his **friends**.

The **crowd** watched in awe, praising God that he had given this man Jesus such authority.

WHOOSH

Follow up

Discussion

- Invite children to share things that frighten or worry them. What do we do when we are afraid or worried? How do we react?
- What can we learn about being afraid from the story of the storm?
- Jesus isn't physically here with us as he was with the disciples. How can we talk to him today?
- How will God help? Will he always make whatever we are frightened of, or upset by, go away?

Activity

- Take a small watertight bottle (a drinks bottle is ideal) and put a small amount of sand or gravel in it.
- Model a boat from clay and add it to the bottle. Fill the bottle with blue water and secure the lid.
- Shake to create a storm and watch as the waves settle again.

Prayer

Father, I am sometimes afraid of _____. Help me to remember that I can talk to you about it and that you are right there with me when I'm frightened. Amen

46

Feeding 5000 people

MATTHEW 14:13–32; JOHN 6:1–21

characters	objects	sounds
Herod Herod's brother wife John the Baptist people Salome guests guards followers Jesus crowds disciples Philip Andrew boy Peter	prison party mountains twelve baskets boat wind waves	screaming

Herod was a bad king. **He** took what didn't belong to him, including his brother's wife. **He** made his **brother** divorce his wife, so that **he** could marry her instead. When **John the Baptist** visited **Herod** to tell **him** that what he had done was wrong, **Herod** had **John** thrown into **prison**. **Herod** would rather have killed **John** instead, but a lot of **people** followed John, and **Herod** was afraid that **they** might rebel if **he** pushed them too far. So **John** stayed in **prison**.

On his wife's birthday, **Herod** decided to throw a huge **party**. Her daughter, **Salome**, was a beautiful dancer and **everyone** enjoyed watching **her**. As **her** dance came to an end, **Herod** was so pleased that **he** promised that she could have anything she wanted.

'Anything at all?' **she** questioned. When **Herod** confirmed that **he** really did mean anything, **Salome** went off for a chat with her **mum**. Seeing their chance for revenge, it wasn't long before **she** came back to **Herod** and asked for John the Baptist to be killed.

WHOOSH

Now when he said 'anything', **Herod** was thinking of gold, or jewels, or clothes. So **he** had a problem. **He** was sorry that **he** had said 'anything', but, as **he** looked around at his **guests**, **he** realised that **he** had made a promise in front of them all, so there was nothing he could do but order his **guards** to go to the prison and kill **John the Baptist**.

Some of John's **followers**, hearing that he was dead, went to **Jesus** and told him what had happened. Wanting to be alone, **Jesus** crossed Lake Galilee to go somewhere quiet, away from everyone. But when **he** arrived, crowds of **people** were there again, **some** waiting to hear him teach and **some** waiting to be healed. **He** felt so sorry for them that **he** healed everyone there who was sick.

WHOOSH

Even when **Jesus** walked up into the **mountains**, **people** followed **him** to listen to him teach. As evening came, the **disciples** came up to Jesus, looking worried.

'We're miles from anywhere,' **Philip** said. 'Send the people home so that they can buy some food.'

'Could we feed them?' **Jesus** asked him.

'Hardly,' answered **Philip**. 'It would take a year's wages just to buy a little bit of bread for everyone.'

Then **Andrew** joined in the conversation.

'Well, there's a **boy** here with five barley loaves and two fish,' **he** said, shaking his head as he realised that it wasn't going to go very far by the time it had been shared out.

WHOOSH

The ground around them was very grassy, so **Jesus** told the **disciples** to sit **everyone** down. By the time the **disciples** had organised everyone, **they** reckoned there were about five thousand people there. Then, **Jesus** took the five little loaves from the **boy**, **thanked** God for them and **broke** them into pieces. **He** did exactly the same with the fish. When the **disciples** started passing the bread and the fish around, they found that there was plenty for **everyone** to eat. When **everyone** was full, **Jesus** told his **disciples** to go round and collect all the leftovers, so that nothing was wasted. To their amazement, they filled **twelve baskets** with all that was left.

WHOOSH

Everyone was talking about the miracle as they made their way home. 'This must be the Prophet,' **they** agreed with each other. **Jesus** made his **disciples** get into a **boat** and **start** sailing back across the lake, but **he** waited until he had sent all the **crowds** away. When **they** had gone, he went further up on to the **mountain**, because **he** wanted to be alone to pray.

Meanwhile, the **disciples** were finding it hard to get home. **They** were sailing against the **wind**, and the **boat** was being tossed around by the waves. Just before dawn broke, **they** looked out across the lake and saw **Jesus** coming towards them, walking on the water. **They** were terrified and, **thinking** that he was a ghost, started **screaming**.

WHOOSH

'Don't be afraid,' **Jesus** said to them straight away. 'Look, it's me, Jesus.'

'If it's really you,' **Peter** called, 'tell me to come to you.'

'Come on, then,' said **Jesus** in reply, and **Peter** got out of the **boat** and started walking on the water towards **Jesus**. While **Peter** was looking at **Jesus**, he was fine, but, as soon as **he** started looking around at the **waves** and fretting about how strong the **wind** was, **he** started to sink.

'Save me!' **Peter** shrieked in fear, and **Jesus** reached out his hand and took hold of **him**. 'Why do you doubt?' **he** asked, as **they** got into the boat together and **sailed** to the shore.

The next day, the **people** were back again, asking **Jesus** for some more bread. 'I am the bread of life,' **Jesus** told them. 'Anyone who trusts me will never be hungry or thirsty again.'

This time, **many** of the people wandered away, grumbling. 'What does he mean?' they asked. 'He's only Joseph's son.'

WHOOSH

Follow up

Discussion

- What might the disciples have thought when the bread and fish fed so many people?
- Why did Peter start to sink?
- What did Jesus mean when he said that he was the bread of life?
- Why didn't people believe in Jesus, even though they had seen him performing miracles?
- Why do people today choose not to believe in Jesus?

Activity

- On the outside of a paper sandwich bag, write and decorate Jesus' words, 'I am the bread of life'.
- Make five loaves and two fish to put inside the bag. Depending on the time available, these can be drawn and cut from card, or modelled.

Prayer

Father, help me to understand what Jesus meant when he said that he is the bread of life.
Amen

47

Healing the blind

MATTHEW 8:1–4; 20:29–34; MARK 1:40–45; 10:46–52;
LUKE 5:12–16; 17:11–19; 18:35–43; JOHN 9:1–41

characters	objects	sounds
Jesus people man with leprosy priest ten men with leprosy blind man disciples neighbours Pharisees Bartimaeus	temple village Siloam Pool	

Everywhere that **Jesus** went, he was met by **people** who had come to him to be healed. On one occasion, after **Jesus** had spent all day sitting on a mountainside teaching **people**, **he** was even followed by the **crowd** as **he** walked home.

Suddenly, a **man** appeared in front of him and knelt down on the ground.

'Lord, if you want to, I know you have the power to heal me,' he said.

Jesus looked at the **man**. He was covered in leprosy, a skin disease that was so infectious that nobody was allowed to touch him in case they caught it, too. But **Jesus** reached out his hand and touched him anyway.

'I want to make you better,' **he** said, 'so now you are well.'

At once, the leprosy disappeared. **Jesus** told the **man** to go to the **priest** to show him that he was well again, and then to take a gift to the **temple** to say thank you to God that he had been healed.

As the **man** was leaving, **Jesus** said, 'Don't tell anyone what's happened. Just go straight to the priest.' But the **man** was so excited that he just couldn't keep the good news to himself. He told so many **people** that **Jesus** was swamped by an even bigger crowd, wanting to see this miracle worker.

WHOOSH

Another day, **Jesus** was walking along the shore of Lake Galilee, on his way to Jerusalem. As he went into a **village**, **ten men** came towards him. **They** stopped some distance away from him and **Jesus** could see that they all had leprosy.

'Jesus, please have pity on us,' **they** shouted to him.

Jesus looked at them, and then **told them** to go straight to the **priest**. As **they** went, **they** were healed. They looked at their skin in amazement. When **one** of the men realised what had happened,

he turned straight round and rushed back into the **village** to find Jesus. All the way there, **he** was leaping and jumping and shouting praise to God.

When **he** found **Jesus, he** knelt down in front of **him**, and just **said**, 'Thank you, Lord.'

'Weren't there ten of you that I healed?' **Jesus** asked. 'Where are the other nine? Why are you the only one who has come back to say thank you?'

And then **he** told the man to get up. 'Your faith has made you well,' **he** said.

WHOOSH

As **Jesus** was walking along one day, **he** saw a **blind man** begging at the side of the road. The **disciples** started wondering why the man was blind. Was it because of something he had done wrong? **Jesus** stopped and said to them, 'You will see God work a miracle for this man.' Then **he** spat on the ground, made some mud and smeared it across the **man's** eyes.

'Go to the **Siloam Pool**,' **he** told the man, 'and wash off the mud.' So the **man** did as he was told, and, after **he** had washed off the mud, **he** could see for the first time in his life. His **neighbours**, who were used to seeing him begging, actually wondered if it was the same man.

'Yes, it's me,' **he** told them, and explained what Jesus had done. 'I was blind, but now I can see.'

But the **Pharisees**, who had seen what happened, weren't happy. Who was this man Jesus, who was healing people? And worst of all, what was he thinking of, healing people on the sabbath? It was against the rules.

WHOOSH

Bartimaeus was also a blind man. **He** was sitting where he sat every day, by the side of the road, begging. But one day things were a bit different—the day when **Jesus** was walking to Jericho. There was a **crowd** gathering and, when **Bartimaeus** heard their voices, **he** asked what was happening.

'It's Jesus of Nazareth,' **they** said. 'He's about to walk past us.'

Bartimaeus couldn't see Jesus but **he** could certainly make sure that **Jesus** saw him!

'Jesus, son of David, have mercy on me,' **he** shouted, over and over again. **People** kept telling him to be quiet but **he** just kept on shouting even more loudly, 'Jesus, have mercy on me.'

Hearing the voice, **Jesus** stopped and asked **someone** to lead the **blind man** out of the crowd to where he was standing.

'What's going on?' asked **Bartimaeus**. When **he** heard that Jesus was asking for him, **he** threw off his coat and jumped up, ready to be taken to Jesus.

'What do you want me to do for you?' **Jesus** asked him as he got near.

'I want to see,' **he** said simply.

'You can see,' **Jesus** said. 'Your faith has healed you.' And sure enough, **Bartimaeus** could see, and **he** set off down the road, walking alongside **Jesus**. When the **people** in the crowd saw what had happened, **they** started shouting praise to God along with **Bartimaeus**.

WHOOSH

Follow up

Discussion

- Why were the Pharisees unhappy?
- Why do you think the nine lepers forgot to say thank you?
- How did Bartimaeus say thank you?
- Do we ever forget to thank people when they have done something for us?

Activity

- Take two face-sized circles of card. On one, draw a sad face with closed eyes. Glue wool on to the face for hair and a beard.
- On the second circle, draw a happy face with open eyes, and glue on some hair and a beard.
- Glue the two circles together to show Bartimaeus before and after he was healed.

Prayer

Father, thank you that you care about people who are ill or sad. Help me to help other people and to say thank you when someone has helped me. Amen

48

Jesus heals more people

MATTHEW 9:18–26; MARK 5:21–43; LUKE 5:17–26; 8:40–56; JOHN 5:1–13

characters	objects	sounds
Pharisees	house	
teachers of the law	city gate	
Jesus	pool of Bethesda	
people	five porches	
friends	water in the pool	
man on mat	Jairus' home	
sick and crippled people		
healed man		
Pharisees		
Jairus		
crowd		
Jairus' daughter		
Peter		
woman		
messenger		
James and John		
family and neighbours		
child's mother		

The **Pharisees** and **law teachers** were listening to **Jesus** teaching: **they** had travelled from all over Galilee and Jerusalem to listen to him. **They** were getting annoyed that **Jesus** seemed to have the power to heal sick **people**, and, while **he** was speaking, a group of **friends** appeared, carrying a **man** on a mat. The **man** was crippled, and his **friends** wanted **Jesus** to heal him. **They** tried to take him into the **house** where Jesus was, but, because of the huge crowd of **Pharisees** and **lawyers**, **they** couldn't get anywhere near **Jesus**.

So instead, **they** climbed up the steps that led to the roof of the house. **They** removed some of the tiles and then **they** carefully let the **man**, still lying on his mat, down through the roof until **he** landed on the floor in the middle of the room.

'My friend,' **Jesus** said when he saw him, 'get up and walk.' And straight away, the **man** got up and started walking away.

WHOOSH

Jesus was in Jerusalem for a festival. Near one of the **gates** to the city there was a pool of water known as **Bethesda**, with **five porches** around it. Lying under the roofs and propped up on the columns that supported the porches were all sorts of **sick** and **crippled people**. Every so often, the **water** in the pool would start to stir, and **people** rushed to get into the pool, believing that the first person in the water when this happened would be healed.

One **man**, who had been ill for 38 years, was lying beside the pool. Knowing how long he had been there, **Jesus** went over to him.

'Don't you want to get better?' **he** asked. And the **man** explained that **he** had nobody to help him into the water, so whenever **it** started to stir, **someone else** always got there first.

'Pick up your mat and walk away,' **Jesus** said, and the **man** was healed. **He** stood up, **leaned** over to pick up the mat on which he had lain for so many years, and then **he** started walking around. **He** looked around to speak to Jesus, but **Jesus** had already left.

WHOOSH

'Why are you carrying a mat?' asked a stern **voice**. 'Don't you know that it's against the rules to carry a mat on the sabbath?' One of the **Pharisees** started making his way towards the man.

'Oh, the man who healed me told me to do it,' **he** answered.

'Who said that?' asked the **Pharisee**. When the **man** told them that it was Jesus, the **Pharisees** got really angry and started making trouble for Jesus because he had broken the rules about the sabbath.

WHOOSH

One day, as **Jesus** got out of a boat on the shore of Lake Galilee, a **man** pushed his way out of the **crowd** and knelt down in front of Jesus. His name was **Jairus**. He was an important Jewish official and **he** had been waiting for Jesus because his twelve-year-old **daughter** was dying. He desperately wanted **Jesus** to go with him to his **home** to heal **her**. **She** was his only daughter and he loved her very much.

As **he** begged and pleaded, the **crowd** around them got bigger and bigger.

'Who touched me?' **Jesus** asked suddenly.

People looked at each other: what a strange question! Lots of **people** were pushing around him—of course someone had touched him. Lots of people, probably.

'Master, there are a lot of people crowding around,' **Peter** said to **Jesus**, while everyone was saying, 'Well, it wasn't me!'

'I felt power leave me,' said **Jesus** and, as **he** said this, a trembling **woman** appeared and knelt in front of him. **She** told **Jesus** that it was she who had touched him. **She** had been ill for twelve years, and **she** knew that she only needed to touch the hem of his cloak and **she** would be healed.

'Go in peace,' **Jesus** said to the **woman**. 'Your faith has made you well.'

Jairus was waiting anxiously for Jesus to go with him, but while **Jesus** was talking to the woman, a **messenger** came up to **Jairus**. He had come from Jairus' home.

'You don't need to bother the teacher any more,' the **messenger** said. 'Your **daughter** is dead.'

WHOOSH

'Don't be afraid,' **Jesus** said to **Jairus** as they started walking, indicating to **Peter**, **James** and **John** that they were to go with him. 'Have faith and she will be well.'

When **they** arrived at the house, **Jesus** found **family** and **neighbours** crying and weeping, making a terrible noise.

'She isn't dead; she's asleep,' **he** told them all as **he** sent them all outside. Then, together with her **father** and **mother**, and his **three disciples**, **Jesus** went to where the girl was lying. 'Get up, little one,' **he** said, as **he** took her by the hand. And **she** got straight up.

'Give her something to eat,' **Jesus** told her **mother** as **he** left.

It wasn't long before news of what had happened spread from **person** to **person** for miles around.

WHOOSH

Follow up

Discussion

- How many people in this Whoosh came to Jesus with a problem?
- What did they have to do before Jesus helped them?
- What did Jesus do then?

Activity

- Cut nine strips of paper, each 2.5 cm wide and 30 cm long. Cut nine more strips in a contrasting colour, each 2.5 cm wide and 22 cm long.
- Weave the strips together to make a mat, securing the edges with glue.

Prayer

Thank you, Father, that we can come to you with problems and ask for help, knowing that you love us. Amen

49

Being humble

LUKE 18:1–30; 19:1–10

characters	objects	sounds
disciples Jesus judge widow two groups of people Pharisee tax collector parents children rich man Zacchaeus	court temple sycamore tree house	

The **disciples** were asking **Jesus** about praying. He wanted them to understand that they should never give up praying, so **he** told them a story.

Once there was a proud **judge** who didn't care about God, justice, or being fair to the people he was judging in **court**. There was also a **widow** in the same town, who knew that **she** had to go to **his court**. So **she** paid him a visit.

'Make sure I'm treated fairly in your court,' **she** told him, but the **judge** refused to do anything about it. So the **widow** kept going to see him.

'Make sure I'm treated fairly in your court,' **she** said, **every** time she saw **him**. Eventually **he** couldn't stand **her** nagging any more. **He** didn't care about God's rules and **he** certainly didn't care about justice, but **he** wanted to stop the widow bothering him. So **he** helped her out, just to get rid of **her**.

So, **Jesus** explained, if a dishonest judge helped someone who kept on asking, think how much more quickly God will help people who cry out to him, because he loves them.

WHOOSH

One day, **Jesus** heard some people talking. **They** thought they were much better than others, and it was obvious that **they** looked down on **people** who weren't like them. **Jesus** told them a story to help them understand how God sees people.

Two men went to pray in the temple. One of them was a **Pharisee**, an important person in his community and a man who made sure that he kept all the rules. **He** liked to boast as well, to make sure that **people** knew how good he was. The other was a **tax collector**, a person who was hated by everyone.

The **Pharisee** stood by himself in the **temple** where he could be seen by **everyone. He** looked up to heaven and prayed, 'Thank you that I'm not greedy or dishonest, like some people. I'm so glad I'm not like that tax collector over there. I'm so good that I fast two days a week and give one tenth of all my money to the temple.'

The **tax collector** didn't think he was good enough even to look up to heaven, so **he** stood where he couldn't be seen, with **his** head bowed. **He** thought of the things he had done wrong, things that had broken God's rules for living. 'Have pity on me, God,' **he** pleaded, 'because I am such a sinner.'

As the **two men** left the **temple, Jesus explained**, it was the tax collector who God was pleased with. **He** was humble and knew that he was a sinner.

'If you put yourself above others,' **Jesus** ended, 'you'll be brought down.'

WHOOSH

Afterwards, some **parents** brought their **children** to **Jesus** because **they** wanted him to bless **them**. When the **disciples** saw them, **they** told the **parents** to go away and stop bothering Jesus. But when **Jesus** saw what was happening, **he** beckoned to the **children** to come to him.

'Don't stop them,' **he** told the **disciples**. 'You have to be like a little child to enter God's kingdom.'

Then a rich and important **man** came up to him.

'Teacher, how can I have eternal life?' **he** asked.

'Keep all the commandments,' **Jesus** answered.

'I've kept all of them since I was a child,' the **man** answered.

'Then go and sell everything you have and give the money to the poor,' **Jesus** told him. At that point, the **man** walked away sadly. **He** was very rich and **he** didn't want to part with his money before he followed Jesus.

WHOOSH

Jesus walked on through Jericho. There was a man living in the town, called **Zacchaeus**. He was a **tax collector**, and everyone hated him because **Zacchaeus**, like all tax collectors, demanded more money than was fair, so that they could get rich themselves. **Zacchaeus** was very rich. When **he** heard that **Jesus** was coming, **he** badly wanted to see him, but there were **crowds** of people and, because **he** was short, **he** couldn't see over their heads. **He** tried, but there were too many **people**, and when **he** tried to push his way to the front of the crowd, **nobody** would let him through.

Zacchaeus was so keen to see Jesus that he ran to a sycamore **tree** and climbed it. But when **Jesus** got there, **he** stopped right underneath the tree. 'Zacchaeus,' **he** called out, 'come down out of that tree. I want to visit your house.'

WHOOSH

So down scrambled **Zacchaeus**, and off **he** went with **Jesus** to his **house. People** were scandalised.

'Doesn't Jesus know who this man is?' **they** grumbled. 'He's a sinner, and Jesus is going to have a meal with him.'

But later that day, **people** were even more amazed. **Zacchaeus** had made **Jesus** a promise, and **he** intended to keep it. **He** gave half of everything he had to the poor, and then **he** gave back the money that **he** had taken from **people** unfairly. But **he** didn't just give them back the money he owed; **he** gave them back four times as much.

'I came to look for people like Zacchaeus, who are lost,' **Jesus** said. 'I came to save them.'

WHOOSH

Follow up

Discussion

- What did Jesus want people to understand about prayer?
- What do you think Jesus said to Zacchaeus at his house?
- How do you think people might have reacted to Jesus when Zacchaeus gave all the money back?

Activity

- Draw a sycamore tree on a piece of paper. Sycamore leaves are star shaped: draw lots of them on the tree.
- Draw the crowd waiting for Jesus to arrive. Hide Zacchaeus somewhere in the tree, and challenge a friend to find him.

Prayer

Thank you, Jesus, for looking for lost people so that you can save them. Amen

50

The woman at the well

JOHN 4:3–54; 7:1–52; 8:1–31

characters	objects	sounds
Jesus disciples woman people from the town Jewish official son servants crowd Pharisees chief priests temple police	town well village water jar home in Capernaum festival of Shelters temple Mount of Olives	

Jesus and his **disciples** were walking home. On the way, **they** walked through Samaria, passing a **town** called Sychar. **They** were tired and hungry, so when **they** came across a **well** outside the **town**, the **disciples** decided to go into **town** to buy some food, while **Jesus** rested by the **well**.

While **he** was sitting there, a **woman** came to draw water. Usually, the women of a town came together, so it was unusual to see one woman on her own.

'Please could you give me some water?' **Jesus** asked **her**. 'I've had a long journey and I'm thirsty.'

The **woman** looked surprised.

WHOOSH

'You're a Jew,' **she** said, 'and I'm a Samaritan. We don't have anything to do with each other. Why are you asking me for a drink of water?'

Then **Jesus** said something surprising. 'If you knew who I was, you would ask me for the water that will give you life.'

The **woman** looked down into the **deep well**. **She** looked at her bucket. **She** looked back at **Jesus**. **He** didn't have a bucket. So how was **he** planning to give her any water?

Jesus pointed to the water in the well. 'If you drink the water I give you,' **Jesus** said, 'you will never be thirsty again. It will give you eternal life.'

The **woman** wanted to know all about this water, and **she** wanted to know how to get eternal life, so **she** and **Jesus** started talking. **She** soon realised that he was a prophet.

When the **disciples** returned with the food, they found **Jesus** deep in conversation with her.

WHOOSH

'When Christ comes, he will explain everything to us,' the **woman** was saying to **Jesus**.

'I am Christ,' **Jesus** told **her**, and when she heard that, **she** jumped up and rushed back into town. **She** was so excited to know that the Messiah was sitting by her well that **she** even forgot to take her **water jar** with her. **She** was in a hurry to tell everyone about Jesus.

It wasn't long before the **woman** returned with a **group** of people from her town who wanted to meet **Jesus** for themselves. **They** asked **him** to stay with **them** for a while, so, instead of carrying on to Galilee the same day, **Jesus** and his **disciples** stayed in the **town** of Sychar for two days to teach, and lots of **people** put their faith in him.

WHOOSH

When **Jesus** returned to Galilee, **he** decided to visit Cana, the **village** where he had turned water into wine at a wedding feast. A **Jewish official** whose **son** was very ill had heard about Jesus healing people, so when **he** discovered that **Jesus** was just a day's journey away, **he** went and pleaded with Jesus to heal his son.

'Come, please, before my son dies,' **he** begged **Jesus**, but **Jesus** didn't go with him. Instead, **he** said, 'Go home. Your son will live.' The **official** believed **Jesus** and set out on his journey back to Capernaum.

While **he** was travelling, **he** saw some of his **servants** coming towards him. 'Your son is well!' **they** said when they reached **him**.

'When did he get better?' the **official** asked.

'His temperature went down at one o'clock,' **they** answered, looking at each other and wondering why the time was so important. The **official** realised that this was exactly the time when Jesus had told him that his son was well. When **he** got **home**, his **family** were so amazed that they all put their faith in Jesus.

WHOOSH

It was time for Sukkot, the **Festival of Shelters**. At the festival, an argument broke out in the **crowd**. **Some** people said that Jesus was a good man, but **others** dismissed him as a liar.

About halfway through the festival, **Jesus** went into the **temple** to start teaching. The **leaders** were surprised at how well **he** taught, and they **asked** each other where **he** had got so much knowledge from, when he was just a carpenter's son from Nazareth. But the **crowd** started arguing again, so the **Pharisees** and the **chief priests** decided to send the **temple police** to arrest Jesus.

'Have faith in me. If you are thirsty, I will give you the water of life,' **Jesus** was saying as the **police** arrived. **They** were so amazed at what **he** said that **they** wouldn't arrest **him**.

'You've been fooled by him too,' the **Pharisees** groaned when **they** returned without Jesus.

The next day was the last day of the festival. Early that morning, **Jesus** walked out to the **Mount of Olives** to pray, before going to teach in the **temple** again.

'I am the light of the world,' **Jesus** told the **people** who had gathered to listen. 'Follow me and you will never walk in darkness.' Then **he** said, 'If you obey me, you will know the truth, and the truth will set you free.'

Many **people** wanted to be his disciples. **They** didn't want to walk in darkness any more. **They** wanted the water of life that Jesus promised, and so **they** put their faith in him.

WHOOSH

Follow up

Discussion

- Why do you think the woman got so involved in a conversation with Jesus?
- What did Jesus mean when he said that he was the water of life and the light of the world?
- Why do people choose to follow Jesus?

Activity

- Draw ten cups on a piece of paper.
- Divide the following verse and Bible reference into ten sections: Jesus said / 'Whoever / drinks / the water / I give / them / will / never / thirst.' / John 4:14
- Write one word or phrase on each cup. Cut out the cups, muddle them up, and rearrange them to read the verse.

Prayer

Father, thank you that Jesus shows us the way to eternal life. Help me to understand what this means. Amen

Colouring-in pages

These pages can be downloaded from
www.barnabasinchurches.org.uk/9780857463807

Get rid of the frogs... I'll let God's people go!

169

Doesn't Jesus know who that man is?
Zacchaeus... come down out of that tree!

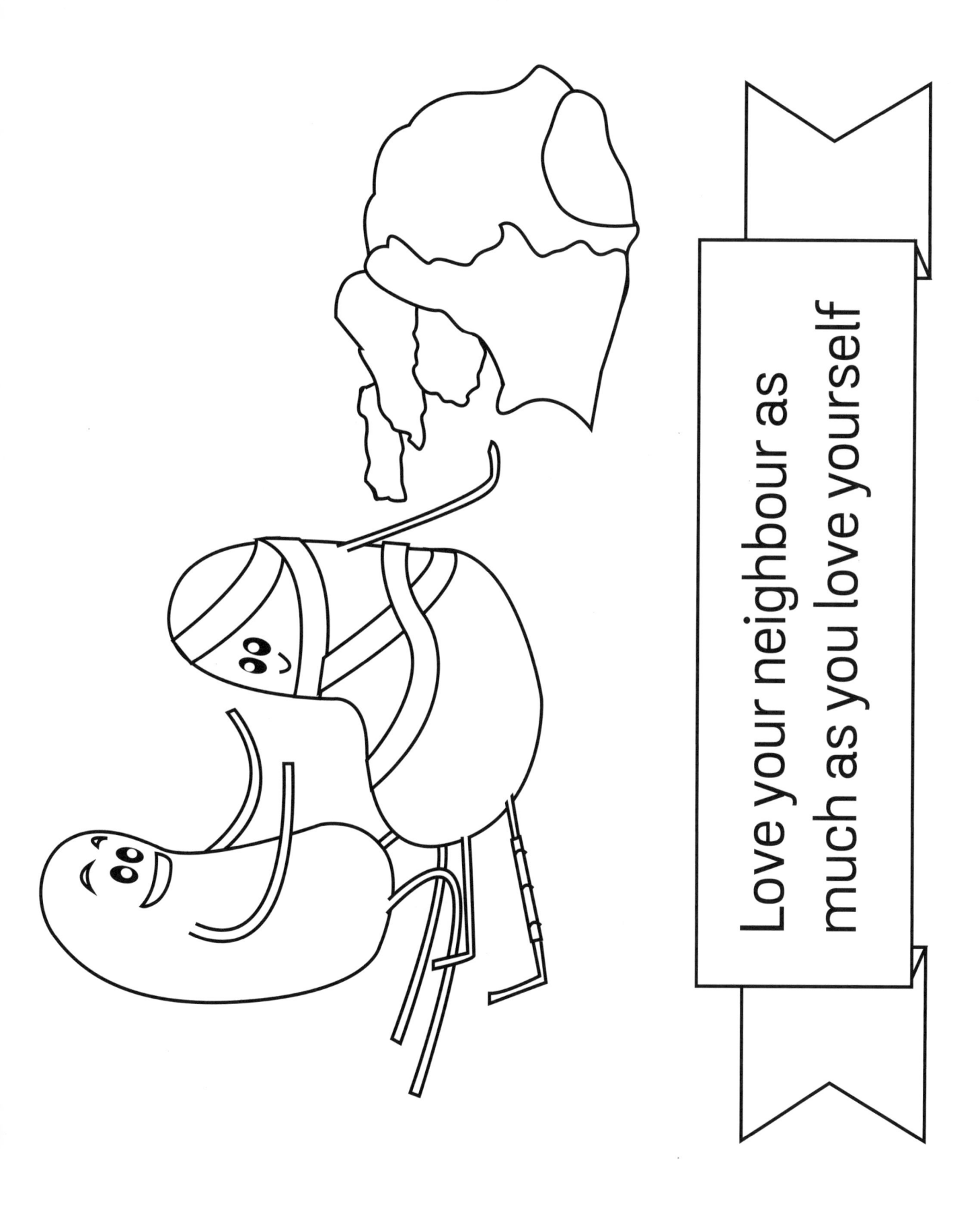

Love your neighbour as much as you love yourself

Go and tell the disciples to meet me in Galilee.

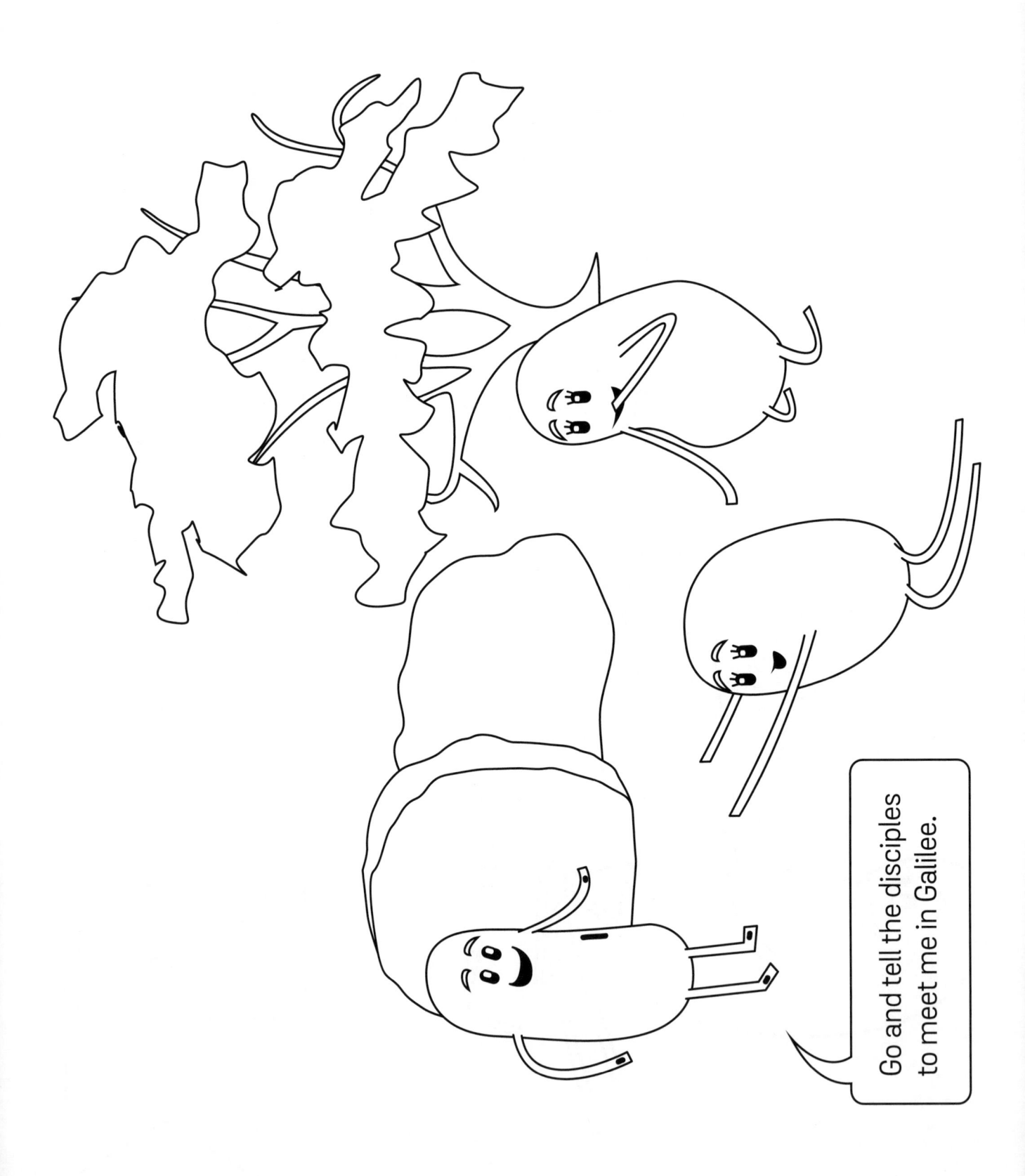

Reproduced with permission from *The Whoosh Bible* by Gill Robins (Barnabas for Children, 2015) www.barnabasinchurches.org.uk

Other resources from Barnabas for Children

The No-Rehearsal Nativity
ISBN 978 0 85746 366 1
£8.99
64 pages

Help! It's the All-Age Slot
ISBN 978 0 85746 023 3
£9.99
256 pages

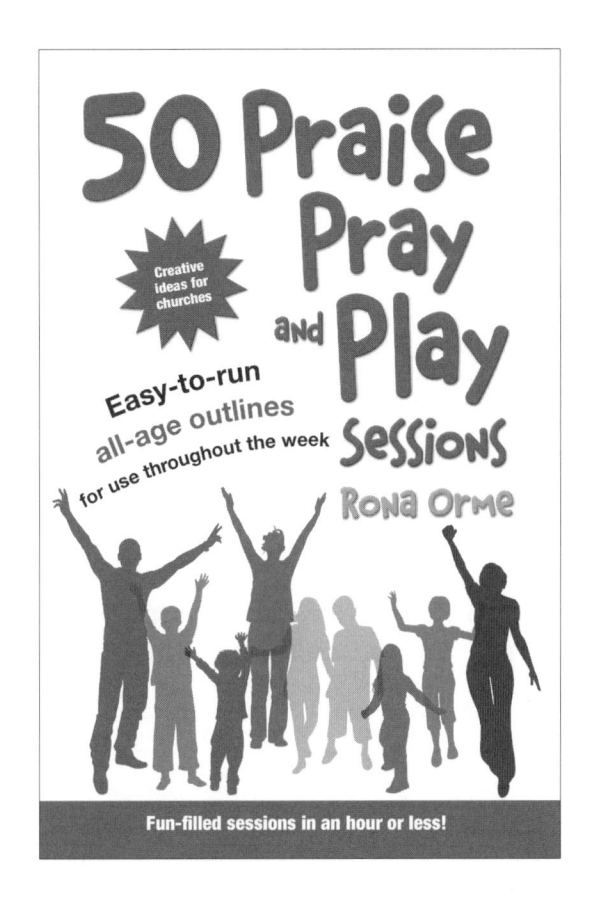

50 Praise, Pray and Play Sessions
ISBN 978 1 84101 662 7
£8.99
256 pages

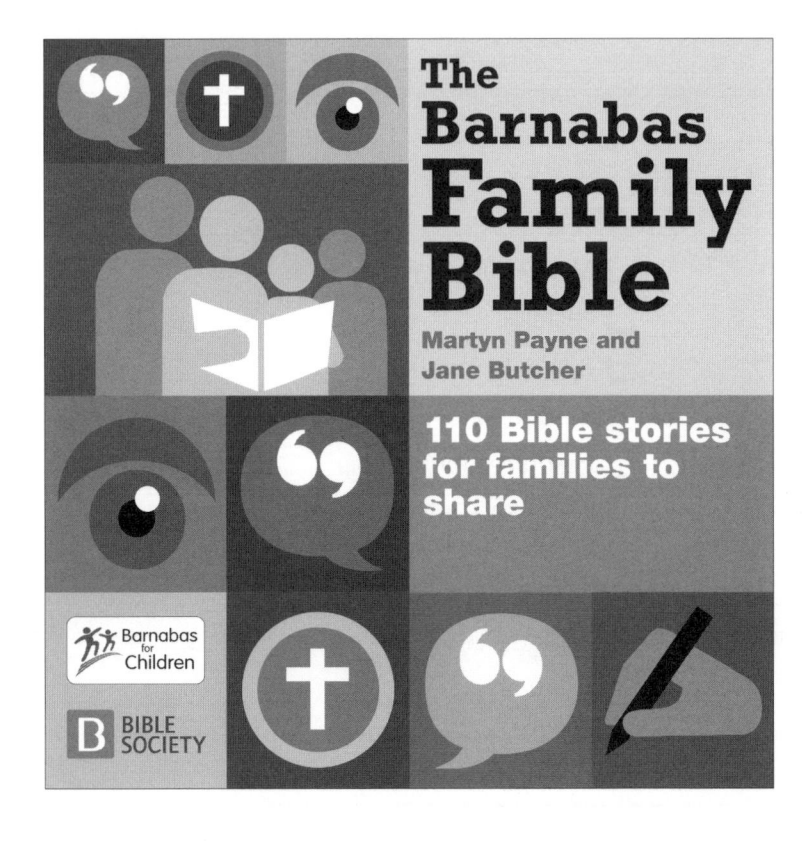

The Barnabas Family Bible
ISBN 978 1 84101 713 6
£9.99
256 pages

Enjoyed this book?

Write a review—we'd love to hear what you think. Email: reviews@brf.org.uk

Keep up to date—receive details of our new books as they happen.
Sign up for email news and select your interest groups at:
www.brfonline.org.uk/findoutmore/

Follow us on Twitter @brfonline

By post—to receive new title information by post (UK only), complete the form below and post to: BRF Mailing Lists, 15 The Chambers, Vineyard, Abingdon, Oxfordshire, OX14 3FE

Your Details
Name _____
Address _____
_____
Town/City _____ Post Code _____
Email _____

Your Interest Groups (*Please tick as appropriate)
☐ Advent/Lent ☐ Messy Church
☐ Bible Reading & Study ☐ Pastoral
☐ Children's Books ☐ Prayer & Spirituality
☐ Discipleship ☐ Resources for Children's Church
☐ Leadership ☐ Resources for Schools

Support your local bookshop
Ask about their new title information schemes.